MUSINGS AT MONT BLANC

MUSINGS AT MONT BLANC

with *Mary Shelley Wollstonecraft*

ROSALINDA RUIZ SCARFUTO

Forest Flaneur Publishing

Contents

Acknowledgements

I would like to thank my family, friends, and colleagues who encouraged me to finish this book despite all odds. Special thanks to TSOEG for inviting me to Mont Blanc for a workshop. I became surprisingly embedded in the landscape introduced to me by Luce in the celebration of the mountain. It was beyond my expectations for which I am grateful. Carlos, my translator, has been kind and generous with his dedication to the project that may have discouraged others between trials and tribulations with Covid, a broken wrist of mine, and arrival of his daughter. Joanna has been such a wonderful eye for detail and supported me throughout the process. Harold has passed away before publication, but his ears were endlessly ready to listen day or night (including re-reading *Frankenstein*) to discuss segments with lively feedback. Mary Wollstonecraft Sr. has been part of my life since university as one of my papers focused on her work. P. Shelley's poems first came to my attention during a visit to a small Italian village above the Poet's Bay on a conference break from Florence.

Lastly, I am utterly indebted to Mary Shelley Wollstonecraft, my muse on this journey. After a deeper reading of her *Frankenstein,* she rekindled in me a profound feminine perspective to Nature and humanity dormant after years of academia. I found her far more virtuoso than previously thought, even surpassing her mother's foundation as a feminist writer due to the complexities of her prose reaching into the heart of darkness of our species, yet brave enough to guide us out. In a fusion of brilliant logic arguing to overcome our zealous ambitions with a sacrifice for the good of all, she offered me light and an escape route. I followed her bread crumbs (incognito) left on the forest floor, high above the raging river Arve that attests to Mont Blanc's melting glaciers; trans-forming my muse's wishes into poetry and splattered paints into canvas. I would like to share these musings beyond my tiny eyes drenched in tears from a collective detour (we have taken together on this planet for worse more than better).

Forward

Mont Blanc & River Arve
R. Ruiz Scarfuto 2019

Wollstonecraft's Frankenstein, partially inspired by Mont Blanc, offers an opportunity to contemplate how humans behave with state-of-the-art-technologies in distinct eras, namely electricity of the 1800s in comparison to digital social networks of 2021. Dr. Frankenstein formulated his 'creature' in a hidden laboratory as a single player, whereas nowadays, a global village participates in social media in open and closed forums.

It could be noted that social networks have fallen into disrepute these days. A place of uncivilised outrage, of agitation. Can we no longer control undesirable developments, such as Victor Frankenstein's creature:

"Had I right, for my own benefit, to inflict this curse upon everlasting generations? I had before been moved by the sophisms of the being I had created; I had been struck senseless by his fiendish threats; but now, for the first time, the wickedness of my promise burst upon me; I shuddered to think that future ages might curse me as their pest, whose selfishness had not hesitated to buy its own peace at the price, perhaps, of the existence of the whole human race."

Is it an invention that we welcomed but are now recoiling from in horror because it can also help spread hatred and ill will? There is an "an 'alteration' in Victor's feelings with the reflection of daylight as Rosalinda Ruiz Scarfuto writes, and we are also tempted to revise our moral judgement in the face of so many problematic cases. Are we like the Sorcerer's apprentice in Johann Wolfgang von Goethe's poem of the same name?

What has been created for our benefit does not leave us unaffected. When we are disappointed, we sometimes go through the stages of shock, denial, anger at our failed creation. We reject it, and yet we are caught up again. That's what happened to Dr. Frankenstein and that's how it culminates in the dramatic ending of the story.

Fortunately, our everyday life is not always as dramatic as our fictions. Still, our anger occasionally obscures our view of the blessings of our creation. For one thing, social networks are often pitiless institutions of morality by means of which we commit ourselves to a life without fault. Humans as social creatures enjoy belonging to communities and rally to defend their own. Albeit at times, this enthusiasm to serve as a watchdog can lead to hatred. Any small errors are made visible through online firestorms.

On the other hand, they are social *media*, hence the bearers of messages, our own messages mostly. Despite this technological creation we are thrown back on ourselves as human beings. And as such, we are capable of conveying love, cohesion, help and much more through our means of media on a daily basis. In these times of a pandemic, it is especially evident. This makes our invention one of a certain moral value, beyond Dr. Frankenstein's imagination.

Mary Shelley Wollstonecraft's literary genius was that she demonstrated how human behaviour was distorted with a superficial love for the female ideal instead of a love that grows over time into a deeper companionship. Social media at its face value has this flaw, too. People have learned since its inception over time to be aware of this deception with superficial friendships or manipulated images. I mean to say, many learned the hard way without any risk management built into the system to guide people or curb this kind of abuse that happens with bullying or harassment. We did not have futuristic literary novels like Frankenstein to warn us in the beginning of social networking. Hence, only in hindsight we have learned. Today, there are more and more initiatives to address the issue of dealing with our media environment at school and to teach digital literacy.

In addition, M. Shelley pointed out that a longing for an ideal friendship that was egotistically motivated, verges on narcissistic behaviour. As she demonstrated in Frankenstein, friendship cultivated an isolation for Victor became obsessive rather than appreciating the people around him. She explains this beauty of human hearts in many circumstances that may or may not have anything to do with personal status or surroundings. It was a warning to branch out and look for the deeper meaning of our fellow humans beyond our mental jails prescribed by culture, education, or even language. Nowadays, social media offers a parallel to her ideas. It is to say, we have been able to benefit from a variety of humans around the globe to augment our perspectives for a richer life of shared value.

Wollstonecraft's laboratory for her own creation was also inspired by the extreme weather of that summer of 1816 and her contact with the landscapes of Mont Blanc. The volcanic explosion on the other side of the globe was considered a natural disaster in the 1800s with its cloud of ashes as a consequence. Unlike the climate change that we face nowadays that is a human disaster. Glaciers are melting around the globe as a consequence of our own behaviour and as a consequence of our inventions.

Social networks again surprisingly offer a multitude of options to connect us to be aware of the approaching fragile tipping point of no return. Young people are following role models such as Greta Thunberg online and are also creating their own networks. Through these means, they are creating new friendships to exchange ideas, actively raise awareness, present resolutions to global environmental challenges including proposals of personal/work habits that can have long term changes to consumption with an awareness raising component that equals the playing field amongst stakeholders including non-humans.

Dr. Robert Gutounig, Graz, Austria 2021

Notebook Chamoix
R. Ruiz Scarfuto 2019

Arve River Frog Stare
R. Ruiz Scarfuto 2019

Prologo

Para quienes ven en el arte algo más que belleza, para los que ven significado y propósito, el arte de escribir es también el arte de la sincronía. Los poemas del Mont Blanc de Rosalinda son hijos de esa sincronía. Nacieron de la visión y el propósito, en un momento dado, y en un lugar concreto, de dos visiones sobrecogedoras: la inspiración de Mary Shelley en el Mont Blanc para escribir Frankenstein, y la sutil y personal percepción de dicha inspiración por parte de la autora.

En un viaje, en un momento del tiempo, dentro del tiempo de la autora, coexistieron el mítico monstruo del libro de Shelley, y otro monstruo, más inasible, más mortífero, más global, el Covid 19. Ese momento del tiempo se mezcla de forma onírica, y a la vez concreta, con la experiencia vital de una poesía muy de nuestro tiempo, donde la plácida realidad que habitábamos con cierta parsimonia se ha roto de forma monstruosa, como la realidad de la novela de Shelley, y como en ella, el monstruo no es solo una aberración qué liquidar, es también la proyección de nuestra sombra, pues la naturaleza, representada de forma limpia y divina por el Mont Blanc, contiene la semilla del misterio de la vida: no podemos alterar los fundamentos de tal misterio, so pena de oscurecer los caminos del espíritu.

La mera relación entre el Covid 19 y el monstruo, hace de este poemario un pionero y un precedente que pasará a conformar parte de nuestra época. La estructura es novedosa, porque es intrépida, al permitirse establecer una relación causal entre una autora conocida (una de las fuentes de inspiración de nuestra autora), nuestra autora misma, y un lugar común que las sobrevivirá a las dos y en el que se resuelven ambas historias: El Mont Blanc de los Alpes, es decir, este mundo, habitado por humanos, hongos, flores, nieve, y a veces, monstruos.

Traducir este poemario ha sido, para mí, una experiencia tan grata como escribirlos, pues eso amerita la traducción. Aún siento el "olor del frío" que me hicieron sentir ciertos pasajes, y veo por sobre mi cabeza las branquias, extrañamente humanas, de los hongos; los horizontes difuminados por la niebla, y la nieve, que, como el desierto, nos invita a reflexionar, si es una sola, o son muchas nieves.

El concepto del tiempo y del destino, juega un papel central, es un eje en torno al cual se suceden muchas de las imágenes poéticas que dan forma al poemario. El cambio, como punto de referencia, sus límites, y nuestra existencia, comprimida, programada, que clama por, cambiar al cambio, que reza y medita porque la realidad, fuera otra.

Rosalinda transita por su memoria, y los Alpes le dan forma a esta. Hay una mirada que recorre tiempos, y quizá haya pasado lo mismo a Mary Shelley, y ese monstruo que confabuló haya sido la pálida sombra del monstruo que alcanzó a ver por esa grieta del tiempo, por esa otra mirada de Rosalinda, en el Mont Blanc.

Tal vez la mutación del porvenir, sea la eternidad.

Traductor, Carlos Torres,
Madrid 2022

Preface (English)

For those who see more than beauty in art, for those who see meaning and purpose, the art of writing is also the art of synchronicity. Rosalinda's Mont Blanc poems are children of that synchrony. They were born out of the vision and purpose, at a given time, and in a given place, of two overwhelming visions: Mary Shelley's inspiration on Mont Blanc to write Frankenstein, and the woman's subtle and personal perception of that inspiration of that author.

On a trip, at a moment in time, within the author's time, the mythical monster from Shelley's book coexisted, and another monster, more elusive, more deadly, more global, the Covid 19. That moment of time mixes dreamlike form, and at the same time concrete, with the vital experience of a poetry very much of our time, where the placid reality that we inhabited with a certain parsimony has broken in a monstrous way, like the reality of Shelley's novel, and like in it, the monster is not only an aberration to liquidate, it is also the projection of our shadow, since nature, cleanly and divinely represented by Mont Blanc, contains the seed of the mystery of life: we cannot alter the foundations of such a mystery, under penalty of darkening the paths of the spirit.

The mere relationship between Covid 19 and the monster makes this collection of poems a pioneer and a precedent that will become part of our time. The structure is novel, because it is intrepid, allowing itself to establish a causal relationship between a well-known author (one of our author's sources of inspiration), our author herself, and a common place that will survive both of them and in which solve both stories: The Mont Blanc of the Alps, that is, this world, inhabited by humans, mushrooms, flowers, snow, and sometimes monsters.

Translating this collection of poems has been, for me, an experience as pleasant as writing them, because that deserves the translation. I still feel the "smell of cold" that certain passages made me feel, and I see above my head the gills, strangely human, of the fungi; the horizons blurred by the fog, and the snow, which, like the desert, invites us to reflect, if it is only one, or if it is a lot of snow.

The concepts of time and destiny play a central role, it is an axis around which many of the poetic images that shape the collection of poems follow one another. Change, as a point of reference, its limits, and our existence, compressed, programmed, that cries out to change to change, that prays and meditates because reality was different.

Rosalinda travels through her memory, and the Alps give shape to her. There is a look that travels through time, and perhaps the same thing happened to Mary Shelley, and that monster that conspired was the pale shadow of the monster that she managed to see through that crack in time, through that other look of Rosalinda, on Mont Blanc.

Perhaps the mutation of the future is eternity.

Translator, Carlos Torres, Madrid, 2022

3

Author's Introduction

Mont Blanc Summit

I am endeared to relate a story that finds me wanton of no more delay, as December 31st is approaching on the close of 2020, a year longer and wilder, than any I can remember of my youth. I am remembering how I walked on the precipices of Mary Shelley's creation; Frankenstein. I discovered that I had begun at the end of her tale, on the banks of the Arve River, that rages through a quaint village of time gone by, called Chamonix. I was astounded at the site of the summit in front of me as I listened to Mother nature roar pass under a calm sky; Mont Blanc stood before me, beautiful and beastly. One may even describe it as an oxymoron, tea tottering between the omnipresent protector for all to see, but in its fissures high up on the slopes, mysterious secrets lurked amongst the shadows. Just over 200 years ago Mary had arrived here on a "six-week tour", where she followed the Arve River to the valley.

Upon first site of both the river and the Mont Blanc summit she and her companion were bewildered, as much as I, at nature's grandeur. With this scene embedded in her imagination, she chose to end her tale of Frankenstein in the crevices of this seemingly forever snowy peak. The two main literary works of Mary Shelley Wollstonecraft are used as references for the texts cited in this book. Firstly, A History of Six Weeks' Tour (1817) that describes her two trips to the Alps and secondly, Frankenstein (1819). Other references are listed in the bibliography.

In late September 2019, as I was following those ramblings, innocently absorbing the poetic inspiration, it was completely unknown to me how the year would end and spill over into 2020, with the silhouette of Frankenstein lying in wait. My recollections of this experience following Mary's footsteps are vivid and wondrous. Back then I meandered along paths and witnessed a colour palette in spectacular hues amongst tantalizing (poisonous) mushrooms, and climbed a rocky ascent to admire an icy sapphire glacier.

Meanwhile, the glaciers were melting at record speed between 2015-2019. As we walked down to an ice cave, the markers in time clearly showed us how much the last four years had devastated the glacier Mary had visited; 100 years previous could not compare. My shock and that of others on the trail reverberated in our gasp! Luckily, in 2020, with the onset of the COVID-19 pandemic, Mother Nature received a reprieve, as tourists were halted at the starting gate. Nature had a vacation from humanity, and we sat back and watched her wonder.

Mary and her companions were confined in 1819 (as I am now in 2020), victims of a volcanic cloud from Indonesia, Mt. Tambora, that delivered a summer with no sun (Geological Society: 2010). She sat at the window in a gloomy atmosphere surrounded by ghost stories, the line between phantoms and life. We too are ending a year of souls slipping away into ghosts, with stories to tell. This is my story of reflecting on the year Frankenstein turned 200 and reappeared in my imagination under a cloud of global warming. In late 2020 I am confined by a host of mutating viruses, but my memories of this journey in 2019 carries me back to that wonderland of colours and poetry inspired by Mount Blanc and Mary Shelley Wollstonecraft.

Rosalinda December 2020

4

Ode to Mary (Shelley) Wollstonecraft

Dear Ms. Mary Shelley,
Wife of a famous poet,
Truth be told, your true lineage,
hidden, under skirts of chores,
Daughter of an architect
of feminist core--- *The Vindication of the Rights of Woman*
Never shall we forget your birth mother,
Mary Wollstonecraft, Sr.

Although *she* suffered death,
before you were a toddler---in your heart *she* grew
unknown to none, not even you,
until your father, Godwin,
penned a memoir, a disruption
setting a course transparent,
her feminine quest uncovered.

A thunderous summer doom,
After ghost stories ignited
The ring of fire in your Soul,
Erupted, the lava surfaced
Rolled over your pillow,
Drenched in blacken ash,
You woke, ignited woman,
To push the pen, dip into
the abyss of the ink well
a black hole, of thoughts,
arranged from chaos,
vitalism vs. naturalism---
mutability exposed.

That very night, compelled
To capture---the devasting omen---
A tale began to unravel,
Dr Frankenstein's daemon was born
In a laboratory, in Ingolstadt,
Despite, a place of *Illuminati*
we had borne a consequence,
Enlightened by lightning!
Mother Nature Spoke
 to Her daughter, Mary.

A familiar memoir,
of generations, of wombs, of women,
who bear and bore the family life,
chores undone, and overdone.
Suddenly, SKY had opened,
Summoned *you*, Mary
To be granted, Time
mundane, undone, left behind,

To scribble,
To ripple,
on the Lake outside,
your window,
turning the tide,
on shores beyond.

I followed, that tide,
Ebb and flow
from the moonlight glow,
behind *your* footsteps.
I, bore the harshness of *our* trail,
carved out by you
and generations before,
beaten breath on breath,
we gasped for air, held down
by mundane, chores.
Ripping free from its grip,
Fantasising vigorous,
Fresh air, streaming,
bursting, into *our* tiny lungs.

Walking in your footsteps,
Beneath, Mont Blanc,
I finally reached out,
To pointed pinnacles,
A glacier you once wrote
so eternal, so splendid,
But now, in front of me,
Just beyond my toes,
A melting pyramid,
Standing firm, dignified,
even though losing its battle.

Its *fresh* waters
transformed,
transfigured,
my dripping sweat,
my salty tears,
Oh Glacier, Oh Mary

I had not known you,
Truly, as I do today!

I concede.

5

Oda a Mary (Shelley) Wollstonecraft

Querida Señora Mary Shelley
Esposa de un poeta famoso
La verdad sea dicha, tu verdadero linaje
oculto bajo faldas de quehaceres
Hija de arquitecto
raíz feminista, vindicación de la mujer
(así, es flecha, tiene más poder)
No hemos de olvidar nunca a tu madre

doña Mary Wollstonecraft (Sr.)
Aunque ella sufrió la muerte
 antes de que fueras párvula
en secreto creció en tu corazón
incluso para ti
hasta que Godwin, tu padre
compuso una biografía, una rotura
marcando un rumbo transparente
su flagrante búsqueda de lo femenino destapado

Un destino de verano atronador
que tras historias de fantasmas
Encendieron el anillo de fuego en tu alma
hicieron surgir la lava
Alrededor de tu almohada
permeada en negra ceniza
Despertaste una mujer encendida
Para empujar la pluma hacia el abismo
del venero de tinta
un agujero negro de ideas
ordenado desde el caos
vitalismo contra naturalismo
vulnerable mutabilidad

Esa misma noche obligó
fuiste conjurada a capturar un mal presagio
Una historia comenzó a desenredarse
El demonio del Dr. Frankenstein había nacido
En un laboratorio de Ingolstadt
Después de todo un lugar Illuminati
habíamos soportado una consecuencia,
¡Iluminado por un rayo!
La madre natura le habló
a su hija, María.
Una memoria familiar
de generaciones, de vientres, de mujeres,
que soportan el hastío de la casa
que haceres deshechos y rehechos
de repente el cielo se abrió
convocándote Mary
para concederte el tiempo
Mundano, dejado, por hacer
Para garabatear,

Ondas expansivas
Allá en el lago,
Tu ventana,
Cambiando la marea,
Más allá de las costas

Seguí a esa marea
fluctuando
desde el brillo lunar
tras *tus* pasos
soporté la dureza de nuestro rastro
tallada por ti
y por generaciones previas
aliento tras aliento agotada
jadeamos por aire, retenido
por quehaceres mundanos
Liberándonos de su yugo
fantaseando vigorosas
fluyendo al aire fresco
que estalló en nuestros pequeños pulmones
Caminando sobre tus pasos
Bajo el Mont Blanc
alcancé finalmente
sus cumbres afiladas
Un glaciar sobre el que una vez escribiste
Tan eterno, tan espléndido
Pero ahora, frente a mí
Justo más allá de mis dedos de los pies
Una pirámide se derrite
firme, digna
a pesar de perder su batalla

Sus aguas *dulces*
transformadas
transfiguradas
mi goteo de sudor
mis lágrimas saladas
Oh Glaciar, Oh María

no te había conocido
realmente, como hoy lo hago
Lo admito.

6

Mary's First Encounter

First Encounter Mount Blanc: Mary Shelley

Mary describes a remarkable tale of her discovery of Mount Blanc, which at first seems fantastical given the terrain she and her four companions covered. Surprisingly she describes this feat in a short diary called, "History of Six Weeks Tour". After leaving Paris, her husband (poet Pierce Shelley) sprained his ankle, giving him priority to ride the mule that had been reserved for luggage and the women if they had tired from walking. Wollstonecraft relates her experiences, accompanied by dubious guides, of an arduous path on foot through unfamiliar landscapes and hardships (hunger, cold, weary limbs). As they pass devastated villages burnt from war, Mary is a keen observer of the devastation. Furthermore, she comments on the behaviours of local people positive and negative, including notes on equality issues.

In a lighter mood, Mary delightfully comments on the flora and fauna at her feet and in her vicinity during her travels, while at the same time she is mesmerized by Mount Blanc in the distance as a compass point that stands out amongst the Alps. She calls the mysterious summit, "Queen of the Aiguilles", and it becomes an attractive focal point in her diary as she ends her first adventure in 1814, having never reached that final destination. Two years later in 1816, she continues the diary with a series of letters describing her long-awaited up-close encounter with Mount Blanc and its neighbouring peaks. Once when she was en route to the Chamois Valley from Geneva, beginning with the raging Arve River, she was faced with the mountain's pure essence, and her perspective was transformed. With its ominous presence at first sight, the sheer magnitude of Mount Blanc sent shock waves through her; "I never knew—I never imagined what mountains were before. The immensity of these aerial summits excited, when they suddenly burst upon the sight, a sentiment of ecstatic wonder, not unallied to madness." Striving to reach the origin of the Arve, she sat on a boulder, admiring icy glaciers at its headwaters. Suddenly, she was stunned by the thunderous sound of avalanches cracking nearby that over time have created the deep crevices of the landscape. Confronted with Mount Blanc from this viewpoint and flanked by its shadowy clefts, she describes the summit as, "the god of the Stoics...a vast animal, and that the frozen blood forever circulated through his stony veins."

7

My First Encounter

First encounter Mont Blanc: Rosalinda

I followed Mary's route from Geneva to the Charmoix Valley, where she paved the route with a horse carriage on her second trip to the Alps, foregoing the walking-mule adventure. I found my bus route was a replica of this route. Once in the valley, I too was astonished by the sheer size of Mount Blanc that casts a shadow over the entire village with its snowy peak against the azure sky, just as Mary described in her diary.

On my first encounter with the mountains and Arve River I observed how the river rushed through the village. The bus route did indeed follow the river, but it was not as obvious on my expedient arrival. I noticed it on the return to Geneva as we left the village, and my eye naturally wondered over the river stones and boulders. The approach from Geneva, on the other hand, was focused on the Alps, since from a distance they are incredibly alluring.

Mary's astonishment of the cracking sound of rock separating from avalanches was echoed on my hike up the valley as we paused and listened to this deafening sound. The roar of the mountain takes you by surprise. I traversed the path with a local group of hikers, whose lungs were far more suited for this adventure than mine. It was my exploration of the headwaters of this raging river that attracted me. However, unlike Mary, the glacier has receded quite a bit in the last 200 years and we were far from the valley on our ascent.

Charmoix under Mont Blanc
R. Ruiz Scarfuto 2019

8

Queen of the Aiguilles

Her Majesty Mont Blanc

Thou art peering over us
Austere and present Above, Mont Blanc,
Named long ago. Raging River Arve below slicing out
New territory, whilst You firmly planted
Glaring sky reflecting,
Stark lines between Heaven and Earth
Thou belong more to Thee above, eternal.

As we (minuscule)—tiny creatures engulfed below
More linked to Mother Nature---earth crumbling
Sadly, faster than any of can bear---soon to be
under waters-icy-frozen, melted in a siege.

Shall Thou, Mont "Blanc" remain
As snowy as today in morrow's time beyond?
What shall we call You, then?
Legend of Mont Blanc---once perpetual snow-covered Dome,
Cathedral of the Alps, worshipped long before---

Will Thou be reduced to simple crags with crevices exposed?
Where once the villagers had revered,
Thou as a single mass of Oneness—
Blanket on the hill—protecting,
 Past, ever Present, and Will Be?

I see You, my Queen, here & now---
Perhaps a figment of my imagination
In years to come---

Mysterious, omen---overtakes the scene---
There is no greater presence than Mont Blanc
 in Chamonix,
drawing one's heart to pound,
Gasping at first sight
Truth be told
I could not stop myself
from reaching out
to touch your banks of snow---legendary poetic

Yet, an eerie nightmare ending here
I am exposed to wonder if I will see
footprints left by Frankenstein himself
And his monster, lurking in the shadows?
Buried deep in centuries gone---with
Mary Shelley, Wollstonecraft
A craft of imagination far greater
than the pen or paper
just the tools to blot the ink---
Ink wells, spilt well---
 to tell her tale.

I begin my ascent to ponder---moonlight beams
Stream down on me---If there are remnants of Mary's charm
left in the burrows of the snow-flaked trail,
I hope I find them or at least a sense
Of where to go---

Queen of the Aiguilles
I truly vow to keep Thou art in Heaven---
Raised above the crags with snow and ice
Of beauty splendid in our perpetual streams
Of consciousness, flowing forth,
So be it, Thou waters---spring up rivers,
To quench our thirst to find true poetic muse,
For we are too tiny in our finite world
To contemplate your Infinite--Eternal grace
spread out as the Heavenly blanket,
To absorb our Earthly tears.
Oh, Majesty, "Have mercy on us."

Aiguilles at Mont Blanc
R. Ruiz Scarfuto 2019

9

Reina de Aiguilles

Su majestad Mont Blanc

Vos miráis por encima de nosotros
Mont Blanc en lo alto, austero y presente
Hace tanto proclamado.
Abajo el río Arve avanza
bifurcando, rebanando
Territorio nuevo, mientras vos te plantabas firmemente
Reflejando cielo deslumbrante
Marcadas líneas entre cielo y tierra
Vos te debes más a las alturas, eterno
Como nosotros, nimios
envueltas criaturitas en lo bajo
Más apegadas a la madre naturaleza
tierra derrumbándose
Por desgracia, más rápido de lo que cualquiera soporta.
Pronto ha de ser bajo aguas gélidas,
inmóviles, derretidas por asedio
¿Os quedareis Vos, Mont Blanc"?
¿Tan nevado hoy como en el más allá del mañana?

¿Cómo os llamaremos entonces?
Leyenda del Mont Blanc
una vez incesante Cúpula de nieve
Catedral de los Alpes, venerado hace tanto
¿Habrá de Menguar en obvios riscos agrietados?
Donde los aldeanos una vez se postraron
Vos como Unidad total
Manto de la colina que protege
Pasado, siempre presente, ¿perdurarás?
Aquí y ahora os veo Reina mía
Quizás un producto de mi imaginación
en años venideros
Augurio misterioso se apodera de la escena
No hay mayor presencia en Chamonix   que el Mont Blanc
que hace vibrar al corazón
Jadeando a primera vista
La verdad sea dicha
No pude contenerme
y alcé la mano
para tocar tu legendaria,
poética cosecha de nieve
Sin embargo, aquí termina una cruel pesadilla
Me atrevo a preguntarme si veré
las huellas dejadas por el mismo Frankenstein
Y su monstruo, acechando en las sombras
Enterrado en lo profundo de los siglos, con
Mary Shelley, Wollstonecraft
Una artesanía de imaginación, más grande
que la pluma o el papel
justo lo necesario para vaciar la tinta
veneros de tinta bien regados
para contar su historia.
Emprendo la subida para meditar
rayos de luna caen sobre mí,

Si quedan vestigios de la gracia de Mary
dejados en los refugios del rastro de copos
Espero encontrarlos
O al menos la señal de a dónde ir
Reina de Aiguilles
juro guardar vuestro arte en el elíseo
En lo alto sobre picos de nieve y hielo
De bello esplendor en nuestro eterno fluir
Avanzando en la conciencia
Que por vuestras aguas ríos broten
Para saciar nuestra sed de encontrar a la musa
Pues somos tan pequeños en nuestro mundo finito
Para contemplar tu infinita gracia
abierta como la bóveda celeste
Para absorber nuestras lágrimas terrenales
Oh, Majestad, "Ten piedad de nosotros".

The Pine Trail

Pine Scatter
R. Ruiz Scarfuto

Pines Past & Present: 200 years reflection

Mary noted how the immensity of the trees in the area differed greatly from her homeland. She mentions the pine trees on several occasions. Her first observation is near Lake Lucerne: "Groves of pine, chestnut, [sic] and walnut overshadow it; magnificent and unbounded forests to which England affords no parallel." Later as she follows the trail to Mount Blanc she notes, "the ravine, clothed with gigantic pines..." Finally, she is face to face with one of the great trunks of these pines, and reflects; "There is something inexpressibly dreadful in the aspect of the few branchless trunks, which, nearest to the ice rifts, still stand in the uprooted soil." It is a land of pine forests that become the last of the tree line to the glaciers and fill the crevices of the mountains above the valley with dark shadows that muster the imagination.

My encounter with these pines was one of amazement. I was trying to imagine Mary's idea of "dreadful" in their branches. They were immense and seemed to defend the landscape with their massive trunks and branches that reached to the heavens. They were gnarled with scars created to withstand the forces of nature above and below their roots. I was eyewitness to perhaps a second generation of pines that Mary had witnessed on her walks. I followed the path along the river, and the decay of these monstrous trunks was apparent in the proliferation of mushrooms that abounded.

I had been invited to hold a workshop on the Forest Flaneur method of art and poetry. My first explorations of the vicinity were on the footpaths along the forests next to the Arve River on the north end of the village. It was autumn and, rather than focussing on the colours of the leaves that usually attract my attention in this season, I was fascinated with the mushroom outcrops that dotted the landscape. It became a treasure hunt to find the camouflaged fungi, creating for me a true "wonderland" of Alice on an adventure. Of course, the poisonous nature of this flora is quite delicate, and therefore I was reluctant to apply my "tactile perception" to create the palette for this poetic landscape. I observed these mushrooms keenly with my visual perception and concentrated on other elements in the area for tactile perception. I decided to retract my footsteps with a camera, and add a photo collage to the palette.

Spiral Mushroom Wonder
R. Ruiz Scarfuto 2019

A whisper in the Pine Knoll

Breath of Pine,
I feel refreshed
Your roots here, now
so bolden to survive,
reaching deep inside
the Earth, that I am ALIVE!
through the thicket, bramble, ramble
of my mind, collecting every sense
even nonsense fills my body
on this trail,
As I gasp for every breath!

I ask you now:
"Is it true that Mary passed you by?
200 years ago! Perhaps a seedling,
she once saw You?
No doubt You have matured,
beyond my years and hers,
I am humiliated,
For today, You, hold up,

this Mountain, no small feat! Mont Blanc!
From within my body, mind and Soul!
I am humbled at Your feet.
Knotted, gnarled, bark
Trunk of painful marks
twisted years of journey
through, and through
I see, I feel, I listen
To your Soul, Be True.

Towering
over me, a tiny poet,
I am here, far below,
scattered mind
like autumn leaves
randomly
I stop.

Please
speak to me
for only you can tell your story,
true,
For when you fall
I may not be here, no one at all.
Who will listen then?

I lay down
On the Earth
Waiting for response...
a rushing pulse within the roots
begins to pound!
Hear me now *Poet:*

"Sediments

Began to crumble
with every glacier
melting faster than before
across the *seven* seas,
cutting ice like the sacred butcher
warning me, my sisters, brothers
to beware
all the forests, falling down!"

We heard the wind,
Ripping through, our knolls
blowing in our ears,
rattling all our branches,
we feared the end
was near."

A voice began to speak:
'It is hidden in the core,
you must go far beneath,
to find your precious rock
your bedrock in the storm.'

"I dug into the core,
Centre of our Earth
Day by Day
Night by Night
I did not stop
My roots exhausted
But I would not let them rest.
Until I found
My rock, behold!"

"*Mother*, I wept
Help me!

I am tired, broken,
and so frail,
I feel so very lonely,
I haven't even seedlings,
to replace me, when I fall."

"*She* nourished me,
made me stronger
with *Her* precious minerals,
Kept me solid, bold, and strong,
After many months below
She announced:

'Time
for you
to stand tall
Above
as an Elder
of your tribe,
you must call a poet---
To come and dance, again
Around your trunk,
Only then,
the seedlings will
return, and you
can once again
rejoice in birth reborn.
Upon the poets'
lips I will send
my muse
to sing.'

I,
your poet,

called,
today.
My footsteps
summoned
from the bedrock
core?

"The column you see today,
Comes from far beneath
Truth be told,
So Above,
So Below,
So Be it!
I
AM"

Me, the poet,
Suddenly, heard an echo through the roots,
A shock wave pierced my ear
I had to lift my tiny head
To save my brain from bursting forth,
Then suddenly from
High above
Came
A
Voice

"I have waited
For you my *friend*,
a poet of the forest,
I did call you
As my MOTHER said."

I, the poet was confused.

"For I your pillar PINE has not *fallen*
but look I have no seedlings!
My shade is wasted on a barren
trail of runners.
I fear I will but disappear
Forever, leaving you, the poets
With nothing, to inspire.
I had hoped someday
My call would be heard
Even though, it is quite muted
By the rushing waters, melting fast
my bedrock, homeland, siphoned last
reduced, but I refused to quit.
I summoned on the Moon
To spread my call
So, you came
Daughter
of
Moonlight glow.
I, the poet
saw the branches sway
for now, the wind
joined in
the mighty rattle
frightened me
I turned and hugged
My pillar Pine.

"Yes!
Ms. Mary Shelley
wrote of Me! A seedling, once.

She was here, with my friends,
She mingled, mused and laughed
In my father's shade"

I, smiled---with no response,
For fear my ears
May be forever
deaf.

"I am alone,
I am no longer
At the centre of your dance
Where once your mothers, fathers,
brothers, sisters
gathered in sacred clothes
singing 'round my trunk
with seeds on ankles
to celebrate
the season
change."

I felt the pain,
this mighty being---so eloquently revealed
I held on---hoping my embrace
could soothe, a broken heart, so immense.

"OH! I miss
Their Songs of Joy
Turning with the leaves
Once shared, together, you and I
On strings of harps,
On human voice
Rejoicing of the Mother."

I, the poet,
Slowly, reached up, and whispered
In its friendly knoll;

"Oh,
Mighty Pine!
I *am* so sorry
We have forgotten
To sing the songs
upon this mountain face
to honour cornerstones
unseen, beneath your trunk
That every breath, you take,
to push your roots, below
Giveth us the strength to create, to live!
On solid ground
As I gasp for my tiny breath---
On this very trail,
I admit
I had not noticed
An absence of those seedlings,
children of the forest---shame on me!
Your last breath, a call,
your very last!
Expired
Has not gone
In vain."

I, the poet began to dance
Around the trunk
With sacred song
Magically my lips
could sing!
To celebrate

this Pillar Pine
Divine.

I think, I saw
Mother Spider
Crawl out from darkness
Hidden deep within old Pine's knoll
its tiny---legs began to wave,
A-mused, A-mazed
I hope the Pain
Is soothed
Away
Be Forgotten
Knot! (Not),
nought.

I 2

Under the Mushroom Gills

Orange Mushroom Wonderlanding
R. Ruiz Scarfuto 2019

I.

Frolicking along the mountain path---stone by stone
Mont Blanc, a stone's throw away.
Up along---over a bramble, a steady runner's joy---

Passing me with pen in hand taking stock
Of details too small to notice
If you scurry, like a rabbit.
Let them run ragged,
I am content to wallow
In the shadow of a mushroom gill,
For beneath the beaten path---blink you'd miss it!

Nature's harmony---beauty---
A pageant of colours only Lewis Carroll would know
Absolutely psychedelic---I pinch myself---
To be sure I'm still in this reality.

Never never have I been so full of wonder---wonder full!
Teeter totter on my---tiny---scale
profusely abundant, these wonder cakes,
desserts in Nature, displayed for all?
Spreading joy to only those on slower pace:
          STOP, TURN 'ROUND...
Moving back, to glimpse, a slow dance
Watch, how they stand---firm
Apparently, still.
Surely, they are growing
Changing---transforming
          FORM,
FORMED,
 MORPHED
 META,
METAMORPHIC
DE-COMPOSURE (*without* composure)
FORM-LESS
UNFORMED
NO-THING (nothing)

Forrest floor richer
Tumble, a fallen tree
lay down, gracefully
Who heard it?
Pierce the Heart,
not even I wept, for its fall.
Now destined for compost
        Fungi meticulously
Appear, Tasks to finish
 I, a witness
Of a palette richer
orange so vibrant, red so robust
Blinds me so.

II.
I lay down
on the forest floor,
rugged rocks pinch my spine
like the giant Pine, silent.

A pine once seen
By Mary 200 yesterday's ago?

Here, under the mushroom gills
Fascinated, I am
By the world, underside,
upside down, downside up
With my fungi friends.
careful,
tricky
not to touch!
Even *Alice*, took notice of a bottle
Before she lifted the liquid, "Drink me"
Was it labelled, poison?

I am no expert on fatal edibles,
Spores of Poison,
Spread freely on airwaves,
I am not testing,
or wanton to know
by my own experiment.
Ancestors, intuitive,
Listened to Nature's call
Beware! I hear them echo!

Frozen, bending my head, lower
My lips silent, until my own eyes,
Are open, She reveals, her treasure...
Under the Gills---a world unto itself
I gasp!

Delicate
Rigid
Harmonious
Random
flexible
Is there a beauty
So perfectly
Aligned.

So attractive
to 'touch'

NO! I mustn't!

I shy away...
Respecting HER
Underside
Her nameless, jewel

A fine art
gallery
to admire
up close,
but far
from touch!
I dare not to disturb
Whence She sprays me
With her spores---

A mere step out
Of the beaten runner's path
Nature so nonchalant, waiting for us
To slow down,
Ancient, as tainted bronze
On unused urns,
a reservoir of *herstory*---
evolutionary
metaphysics meets biology,
I am captive,
in Her class---a charm bracelet
made of gems,
dotted, hidden, in someone's
country side.

I wake up from my day dream,
Where have I been?
Visiting a foreign land, as Gulliver,
I met the Yahoos, and You!
My mushroom *friends*!
Stepping away, ever so slowly,
As I came---promising,
"Tomorrow I'll be back."

III.

T' was tomorrow
Had I not been
Just here---there?
Under this tree,
Around this bend.
Was it *impossible* to return?
Overnight---the gills have dis-appeared?
She fooled me---Had I been imagining?
Was it a one-way ticket?
Oh please, appear!

She had stamped me
 in the memory gills
 of my mind/nebulous
entity---not even I know where YOU live?

Whoosh---a sudden breeze,
Quickly I step away
        A Flash
        A Neon passer-by
        A Runner, no doubt.
Once more---missing out
Nature's Art!

As I *turned* back
My eye captured
A glimpse---there She is!
So proud, So tall---
amongst Her miniatures.

I slowly move to greet Her
Quietly, I lay down

with golden charcoal
slivers prickly on my forearm
I look up, to Her door,
I am at Her doorstep,
She opens her Heart, "Morning!"
I think I saw her gills twitch?
"Hello again—It's me"
Sun is glinting
Reflecting—my eyelids blink
Once again
 I enter in
Wonderland
Lewis
called her Alice
I call her nothing
We need not speak
I am under
 the gills
                with Her
mushroom
        tribe.

IV.

Time
stops.
I am, no longer human,
I am humane.
Runners, run,
while Poets---pause
Sensing heartbeats---
animate, inanimate
Rocks rumble,

mountains decompose
under the gaze of spore-a-tic, (spores)
She is all dressed up, today.
Her gills all pressed, pristine
Ready for a tea party, I suppose.

I am in a day dreamy mood---
Calm with hues unspoken,
She winks---?

Ah! Must I really *get up*
from down under here?

Mushroom Down Under
R. Ruiz Scarfuto 2019

13

❧

Mary's Glacier Terror

Massive Ice Blocks 1800's

As we read Mary's account of her visit to the glaciers, I note the difference in her descriptions and my own experience in terms of how much melting of the ice has occurred. She writes of the glaciers reaching the valley floor, and yet I had to climb 1000m to reach them. We can appreciate the effect of her visit to Mont Blanc on her inspiration for *Frankenstein*, with every movement closer to the heart of this enigma, that overcame her with creative force. Her bravery to ascend the glaciers in order to merge with their essence is astounding, given her means and role as a woman of her era in 1816. She was equally fortified to walk, hike, or ride a mule on the dangerous cliffs of this rare landscape. Mary was not merely looking at the Alps from afar through her window on Lake Geneva to create her tale, when she woke from a nightmare and scribbled it down. Rather, she had stored all the tactile and visual perceptions in her body. Finally exploding from her subconsciousness, she became the unique writer to fulfil Lord Byron's dare to write a dazzling ghost story. The ending of *Frankenstein* leads readers to roam the North Pole with its endless ice as first perceived by Mary in Mont Blanc, and we are left with a cliff hanger; the 'monster' escapes amongst the ice caps, and she alludes to its presence somewhere amongst us, perhaps even within us. Now in 2019, I write my own tale in the shadows of the ghost of *Frankenstein* 200 years later, a sequel to the original.

The ice glaciers witnessed by Mary Shelley Wollstonecraft in 1816 moved her in a such a manner that they are the most mentioned landscape elements in her diary of visiting Mont Blanc and her story of *Frankenstein*. Her visceral experience was evident in her lengthy descriptions at the edge of the glaciers in the valley of Chamouni at the foot of Mont Blanc, and at the higher point on her ascent to reach the ice pinnacles. She described them as "dazzling", as she was overcome with splendour; and then suddenly with the sounds of avalanches, she was humbled and kept a distance, noting the "desolation" that surrounded the glaciers.

Her imagination begins to unravel as she balances her thoughts between fear and admiration; her diary is overrun with a battle of good and evil superimposed by gods that live amongst the "supreme and magnificent", and at the same time the "violence" that roars in the "dark" crevices. She describes the glaciers as "eternal", with "awful grace", with a reverence of "majesty" seducing her with their "charm". This sets the scenes for the beginning of her tale, *Frankenstein*.

Mary's texts:

"Immense glaciers approached the road; I heard the rumbling thunder of the falling avalanche and marked the smoke of its passage. Mont Blanc, the supreme and magnificent Mont Blanc, raised itself from the surrounding aiguilles, and its tremendous dome overlooked the valley." (Chapter 9-Frankenstein)

"The summits of several of the mountains that enclose the lake to the south are covered by eternal glaciers;" (P. 48- History of Six-Week Tour)

"We did not, as we intended visit the Glacier de Boisson to-day, although it descends within a few minutes' walk of the road, wishing to survey it at least when unfatigued. We saw this glacier which comes close to the fertile plain, as we passed, its surface was broken into a thousand unaccountable figures: conical and pyramidical crystalizations, more than fifty feet in height, rise from its surface, and precipices of ice, of dazzling splendour, overhang the*

woods and meadows of the vale. This glacier winds upwards from the valley, until it joins the masses of frost from which it was produced above, winding through its own ravine like a bright belt flung over the black region of pines." (P. 155 History)

"There is more in all these scenes than mere magnitude of proportion: there is a majesty of outline; there is an awful grace in the very colours which invest these wonderful shapes —a charm which is peculiar to them, quite distinct even from the reality of their unutterable greatness." (p. 155 History)

"The glacier by which its waters are nourished, overhangs this cavern and the plain, and the forests of pine which surround it, with terrible precipices of solid ice. On the other side rises the immense glacier of Montanvert, fifty miles in extent, occupying a chasm among mountains of inconceivable height, and of forms so pointed and abrupt, that they seem to pierce the sky." (p.155-6 History)

"From this glacier we saw as we sat on a rock, close to one of the streams of the Arveiron, masses of ice detach themselves from on high, and rush with aloud dull noise into the vale. The violence of their fall turned them into powder, which flowed over the rocks in imitation of waterfalls, whose ravines they usurped and filled." (P.156-57 History)

"...to visit the glacier of Boisson. This glacier, like that of Montanvert, comes close to the vale, overhanging the green meadows and the dark woods with the dazzling whiteness of its precipices and pinnacles, which are like spires of radiant crystal, covered with a net-work of frosted silver. These glaciers flow perpetually into the valley, ravaging in their slow but irresistible progress the pastures and the forests which surround them, performing a work of desolation in ages, which a river of lava might accomplish in an hour, but far more irretrievably; for where the ice has once descended, the hardiest plant refuses to grow..." (157-58 History)

"The glaciers perpetually move onward, at the rate of a foot each day, with a motionthat commences at the spot where on the boundaries of perpetual congelation, they are produced by the freezing of the waters which arise from the partial melting of the eternal snows. They drag with them from the regions whence they derive their origin, all the ruins of the mountain, enormous rocks, *and immense accumulations of sand and stones. These are driven onwards by the irresistible stream of solid ice; and when they arrive at a declivity of the mountain, sufficiently rapid, roll down, scattering ruin.*

"The verge of a glacier, like that of Boisson, presents the most vivid image of desolation that it is possible to conceive. No one dares to approach it; for the enormous pinnacles of ice which perpetually fall, are perpetually reproduced." (p.159 History)

"Within this last year, these glaciers have advanced three hundred feet into the valley. Saussure, the naturalist, says that they have their periods of increase and decay: the people of the country hold an opinion entirely different; but as I judge, more probable. (p. 159-60 History)

"Do you, who assert the supremacy of Ahriman, imagine him throned among these desolating snows, among these palaces of death and frost, so sculptured in this their terrible magnificence by the adamantine hand of neces-sity, and that he casts around him, as the first essays of his final usurpation, avalanches, torrents, rocks, and thunders, and above all these deadly glaciers, at once the proof and symbols of his reign;"* (p.162 History)

**Ahriman is described as the god of materialism lending a hand to deranged thoughts (R. Steiner).*

"This morning we departed, on the promise of a fine day, to visit the glacier of Montanvert. In that part where it fills a slanting valley, it is called the Sea of Ice. This valley is 9.50 toises, or 7600 feet above the level of the sea. We had not proceeded far before the rain began to fall, but we persisted until we had accomplished more than half of our journey, when we returned, wet through." (P. 162-63 History)

"We have returned from visiting the glacier of Montanvert, or as it is called, the Sea of Ice, a scene in truth of dizzying wonder. The path that winds to it along the side of a mountain, now clothed with pines, now intersected with snowy hollows, is wide and steep. The cabin of Montanvert is three leagues from Chamouni, half of which distance is performed on mules, not so sure footed, but that on the first day the one which I rode fell in what the guides call a mauvais pas, so that I narrowly escaped being precipitated down the mountain."

"We passed over a hollow covered with snow, down which vast stones are accustomed to roll. One had fallen the preceding day, a little time after we had returned: our guides desired us to pass quickly, for it is said that sometimes the least sound will accelerate their descent. We arrived at Montanvert, however, safe." (p.165 History)

"On all sides precipitous mountains, the abodes of unrelenting frost, surround this vale: their sides are banked up with ice and snow, broken, heaped high, and exhibiting terrific chasms. The summits are sharp and naked pinnacles, whose overhanging steepness will not even permit snow to rest upon them. Lines of dazzling ice occupy here and there their perpendicular rifts, and shine through the driving vapours with inexpressible brilliance..." (P.165 History)

"They pierce the clouds like things not belonging to this earth. The vale itself is filled with a mass of undulating ice, and has an ascent sufficiently gradual even to the remotest abysses of these horrible desarts. It is only half a league (about two miles) in breadth, and seems much less. It exhibits an appearance as if frost had suddenly bound up the waves and whirlpools of a mighty torrent. We walked some distance upon its surface. The waves are elevated about 12 or 15 feet from the surface of the mass, which is intersected by long gaps of unfathomable depth, the ice of whose sides is more beautifully azure than the sky." (p. 166 History)

"This vast mass of ice has one general progress, which ceases neither day nor night; it breaks and bursts for ever: some undulations sink while others rise; it is never the same. The echo of rocks, or of the ice and snow which fall from their overhanging precipices, or roll from their aerial summits, scarcely ceases for one moment." (167 History)

Pinacles of Ice

R. Ruiz Scarfuto 2020

I4

My Glaciers Melting

Glacier Decline Shock: 2015-2019

Even though I sat on stones like Mary on the banks of the Arve River in the valley of Chamonix, I was far beneath the glaciers and ice caves that were at least 1000m above me, and hidden from my direct view. Considering Mary's description, I witnessed a vast difference from 200 years ago. Mary writes, "...although it descends within a few minutes' walk of the road...this glacier which comes close to the fertile plain..." and yet I could only imagine these elements. I heard stories of the glaciers and the trails that would lead me to them. I was looking up a sheer cliff of rock ravine cut out by the glacier's path. The two glaciers Mary visited were in two valleys; one was accessible by a vintage train, and the other only by foot. The ice cave that is described in Mary's Frankenstein sounded attractive, so I ventured up on a slow train along with other tourists. Once we arrived, we could walk to the cave on our own down a steep path, or take a cable car. I opted for the walk. However, it happened that the cable car was broken that day; hence, suddenly there was a long line of the ice cave curiosity seekers on my heels. As we descended to the small opening in the glacier's wall of ice, there were markers indicating the years where the glacier had previously receded. The dates were in increments of 100 years, with considerable differences. No one paid much attention to the differences until it came to 2015. The next marker was 2019, exactly 200 years from Mary's visit. Those mere four years showed the same recession of ice as the previous 100 years! The crowd near me gasped and paused with a deep sigh. This reaction was similar to my experience in Hiroshima when we saw shadows etched on a wall at the epicentre of the atomic bomb; tourists suddenly confronted with a phenomenon they had not anticipated. Only walking would one see these markers and realize the tremendous degradation of the ice at such a short interval of time. As we walked away from it there was an echo of silence after having seen that marker. I personally was deeply moved and emotionally devastated even though, in Switzerland just six years prior to this trip, experts had told us on an academic tour that the glaciers were melting faster than expected. I had been walking in three areas of the Alps surrounding Mount Blanc, from the Dolomites in Italy in 1995 to that day in France in Chamonix. Unbeknownst to me, my route over the years had encircled this central figure of Mount Blanc.

Through the centuries tourism in the Alps has been traditionally skiing and hiking. Wordsworth walked in the Alps, and encouraged others from his homeland, as well as other European writers, to do the same. Mary had been following the footsteps of Rousseau and reading his literary legacy of Julie. For Europeans, The Alps have been their Andes, their Yosemite. However, this icon would disappear sooner than expected with such a rapid glacier melt. At the time I had visited in early autumn, there was a frenzy of hikers that were intent on completing an insanely speedy circumnavigation of the Mont Blanc range called, the Tour du Mont Blanc. It is touted as, "3 countries, one identity, 10,000 meters in altitude and about 60 hours of walking, 170 km of discovery for a total of 10 days of satisfaction", crossing the three borders of France, Switzerland and Italy. With the melting of the glaciers and lesser opportunities for ski exploitation, I suppose this type of tourism is the next step to overstepping our boundaries on Nature's soil without time to even contemplate the wonders of nature, or our impact on these wonders.

As I began to tip-toe into the ice cave (slippery), I was silent, lagging behind others to contemplate this truly beautiful wonder. I did feel I was passing into Nature's womb, a forbidden place. Unfortunately, it was set up like some hotel lobby, with ice tables and benches. In the deepest part of the cave, I did find a cubby hole to stand silently as others gazed, raced, and clicked their cameras for instant selfies. I had no camera and recorded the experience with my fingertips, my eyes, and my heartbeat. It remains a visceral memoir, much like my experience crossing an avalanche in the Himalayans 30 years ago. Regarding this particular ice cave, I was dwarfed by her beauty which surpassed my fear of her ice cavern. Now I can read Frankenstein with more affinity to the main character who found solace in this landscape. Mary never writes about the ice cave, but about the pinnacles of the cones of the glaciers. I would have to visit the other valley and hike up to the second glacier to experience her descriptions. I left the "Sea of Ice" glacier which is described in tourist literature as "Mer de Glace, which in the 18th century used to descend all the way into the Chamonix Valley. I was deeply saddened as I went back to my accommodation, as there seemed to be a disconnect in these brochures with the environmental devastation taking place. I had already participated in the typical tourism of visiting Mount Blanc by tram, Mer de Glace by train, flying to Geneve and a bus route to Chamonix. In the Victorian Age, Mary and her companions came here by mules and horse drawn carriages. Today there was much to contemplate about our "advanced" age of tourism, especially when it is described as "walks through valleys carpeted with wildflowers and clinking cowbells."

The next days I thought about hiking up to the Glacier de Argentière which is near the refuge of Lognan at more than 1000m above the valley. I was alone and it was not advised to go up on a solitary mission, so the first afternoon I merely went to the trailhead and asked the locals about the safety of going it alone. They also did not recommend it, but the mysterious glacier was calling me in some strange fashion, so I went back to my room to rethink my plan. I decided to go out on the last sunny day available to me, a Saturday. Perhaps there would be some locals going up for a hike and I could follow them. After the ice cave disaster, I did not want to join another tour. I woke up early, packed light: very small notebook, camera, small thermos, and clothes I could peel off. I went to the trail head and waited. No one was in sight. Then suddenly, a group of 3 men and one woman in hiking gear appeared. With my limited French I indicated I wanted to climb up, but not alone. I asked (gestured) if I could walk behind them and they waved me on to join them. I did not really understand the route on the crumpled paper with a vague outline which I had received from a tourist office!

I discovered immediately that they were swift hikers with significant experience, striding at a good pace. Mind you, they were locals from the area of Mount Blanc. My lungs were no match for theirs! The woman was at the start, with a vigorous stride. I hung out with Bernardo, who kept an eye on me, and we were able to communicate something, as he spoke a little Spanish. It was sheer uphill on the steepest trail I have ever hiked! They wanted to spend the day walking around the glacier, with no time to spare. I stopped briefly at a waterfall, Bernardo snapped a picture, and we continued with a record speed! Bernardo finally gave up one of his Nordic ski poles to me. I was huffing and puffing, but with no sign of giving up! They were all laughing at me. At that point I felt grateful for my light pack. I could hardly step up, let alone carry any more weight! Finally, as we were winding the bend, at the end of the trail of the rock crevice valley, we heard an astounding "crack" that came roaring down from the mysterious heights where the glacier was located. They explained that it was an avalanche and rock crumble; however, it did not stop us from attaining our goal, and we soon reached the Refuge of Lognan! Sylvia, the female leader, wanted to press on, but the other men pulled out some liquor with shot glasses for a celebration, and Bernardo handed out some walnuts! At this point I was flush red, and as I looked up from behind the refuge, I saw the glacier! There were no clouds to block my view. We took some cute photos and raised our glasses to our first leg of the journey. They registered the altitude at more than 1000 m which we did in 45 minutes, my record time in any hiking experience in all my 58 years! As Sylvia urged the group to continue, Bernardo stuffed some more nuts into my hand and pointed out my route to descend. It was the regular trail that was a "slower" path that wound down the mountain to the valley. I would have to do that leg of the trip alone. I followed them to the foot of the glacier and rested there in the sunshine before they departed. Now I was left alone to reflect on this azure conical mass of pinnacles. It was truly astonishing, magical, and breath-taking (literally)! To this day I am in contact with Bernardo, and I hope to revisit my friends in Mount Blanc someday. Who knows their next adventure? The trail down the mountain was long, and those few nuts given to me by Bernardo tasted mighty good during the next 3 hours. On my way down I got lost on the trail in the valley where I headed into back yards, and then I had to backtrack several times. I was ravished with hunger by the time I reached the road, so I took advantage of my last day to splurge on the French cuisine that featured fresh truffles from the forest. I dared not touch those mushrooms when I was on the trail, but gladly tasted them on my plate when served to me by a local chef!

Melting Glacier
R. Ruiz Scarfuto 2019

15

Ice Cave

I am
forbidden follower
of foreshadowed Mary
Forgiven not----
Forebode
Once, a Glacier Sea.

Now, a thawing river dance,
Faster than even SHE, can dance
Exposed---unveiled
As a bride on wedding night
Frightened, frozen,
down, down, down
the mountain,
her dress has fallen
slip sliding away.

SHE, alone,
retreats, here
inside the ICE CAVE!

Deafening glimpse awaits me!
Ignited---Whirling neurons
Massive synapses
doors unhinged,
locks be broken,

My SELF, of frozen
thoughts---dare I step inside?
to break HER silent retreat?

Sapphire,
crystal BLUE
a terrific aura emits
from a side of Mont Blanc,
We have come
To awaken HER
Ghastly proposal
I dare to say.

Above me,
Ice-cycles
hang like tears
Below me,
Ice age
melting years.

YOUR ice-warming Womb,
Sanctum revealed,
Into your cavern,
Shall I roam?

I tip toe,
over fringe of gate,

I gasp!

I am follower
Not too sure,
Down, Down, Down,
the corridor AZURE.

whizzing by,
photos clicking,
selfies---frozen
bye, bye,
birdie,
bye, bye
I sigh!

Dare to touch
YOUR chilling walls
Tap, tap, tap
YOU capture me,
My fingertips,
Sticking
on YOUR icy walls,
My fingerprint,
forever, plastered
in time bygone
I succumb.
moments pass
like hours---
Remember me,
Oh, HOLY ONE!

"WE are ONE,
Poet, you and I.
Amused, and mused"

"WE dance, a dance
Only you can hear!"

Slowly, YOU invite me in
release me, unstuck
my fingers now
are free to wonder
in this cold abode,
to join the mode
of wedding guests
around the floor,
in circles turn,
while I discern,
a piercing sound,
from a chamber
in my heart,
Beating, louder
through my chest...
a long last symphony,
I vaguely remanence.

Exterior---pointed,
with razor edges,
Mary says.
Interior---languid
With dripping wedges
I say.

YOU
pull me deeper
into your sanctum,
Into YOUR icy age
Waves of Beauty BLUE.

I surrender---close my eyes,
I am swimming---in a sea,
La Mer de Glace!
I have arrived!
I am absorbed
into HER womb
I sense a trickle
On my eyelid,
A melting teardrop
Merging, fusing
With my own,
Meltdown complete,
I am re-born.

Frozen in my buoyant dream,
I wake up suddenly,
To foot-steps drawing near.
Mine are stuck,
Wedding guests
mingle here and there,
La Mer de Glace,
Dis-appears.

Where shall
we go
from here,
my wedding friends,
we are all married
to the Groom,
with our carbon
Footprints on the floor,
Of Wedding Bride,
HER womb—wounded dearly so.

Hail Mary, full of GRACE
Forgive us, not?
our sins are at the hour
of our death,
beating away,
drop by drop
My tears---my fears
Withering, even HOPE.

Hold me Mother
For we have sinned!
I reach out.

A Quiet silence echoes
From the BLUE chamber glow.

As the Wedding Guests
Retreat from icy walls,
Blue-blocks of ice
Sheer Beauty
Stunned me cold,
Never had I
been so ashamed,
Never had we
Trespassed so erroneously!

I pause—stand still
A throb in the walls
Pulse---calling me
FREEZE---

I am/ /was/ been
Time relent-less
Marking on

I cannot move--- on
This momentum
Has no U-turn
We are/have/been
Mary and I
Witnesses---
To your weeping walls.

If they call me
To testify
I will tell them
you were once---a *Sea*!

I am sorry,
    We invaded YOUR
    Sacred *Sea*,
    YOUR tears now
    Unstoppable?
    Cutting through the hard rock,
    YOUR sapphire knife,
    gashes blocks of ice,
    Adding to a raging river,
    through the valley, Chamonix
    One day, a village under siege.

    Is it really the finale?
    End of ice age, as they say.
    Once a glacier,
    Stood here and firm---I will say.

    We will *sing* a ballad,
    in your name,
    an Ice Cave Beauty Blue,
    once was here,

Of pinnacles
so sharp
they cut your gaze,
of languid walls,
so smooth,
they made you weep,
unsurpassed, was SHE.

La Mer de Glace!
Glacier Sea!

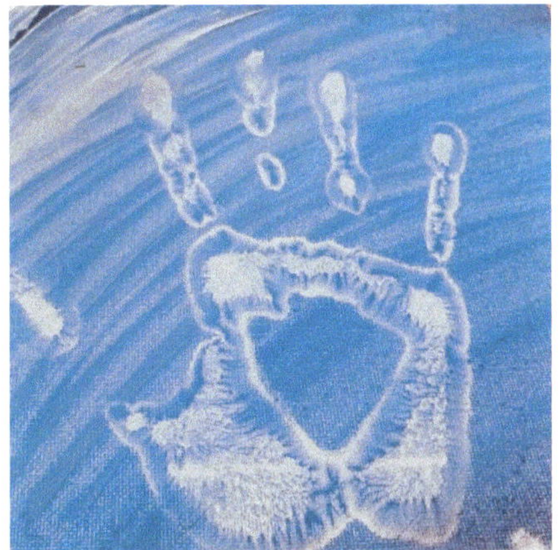

Handprint Ice
R. Ruiz Scarfuto 2020

Melting Ice Cave Wall
R. Ruiz Scarfuto 2020

16

Mary's Eternal Quest

Charismatic chasms (Voyages)

Frankenstein, the novel, begins with a flashback of an explorer at the North Pole, telling his story of meeting Vincent Frankenstein. The descriptions in the letters from a brother to his sister in the fictional character's life make reference to Mary's mental state while on her voyages. She writes about "undiscovered solitudes", images of "eternal" and "perpetual splendour". Mary and her companions are also attracted to a voyage into the deep recesses of the European Alps---Mount Blanc and its glaciers, which have had an illuminous role throughout the ages in the inspiration for literary works. As a result of her trips into the glaciers she discovers the grand difference of admiring the peaks from a distance and the true voyage into the heart of the mountain.

Mary writes:

"...it ever presents itself to my imagination as the region of beauty and delight. There, Margaret, the sun is for ever visible, its broad disk just skirting the horizon and diffusing a perpetual splendour. There—for with your leave, my sister, I will put some trust in preceding navigators—there snow and frost are banished; and, sailing over a calm sea, we may be wafted to a land surpassing in wonders and in beauty every region hitherto discovered on the habitable

globe. Its productions and features may be without example, as the phenomena of the heavenly bodies undoubtedly are in those undiscovered solitudes. What may not be expected in a country of eternal light?" (Frankenstein, Letter 1).

Her novel begins with the overzealous ambition of a North Pole voyage by the protagonist. She incorporates a charismatic charm of Nature intertwined with the childhood dreams of her character that lured him to go beyond his peers and predecessors to reach the unthinkable. She writes of how the concept of a "steady purpose" that "tranquillize the mind", and how "the soul may fix its intellectual eye." Even in Dr Frankenstein's reflection he "dispelled the agitation" in his mind with the foreseeable accomplishment, no matter what the consequences. Mary's own journey was an ambitious undertaking for anyone to embark upon in the aftermath of worn-torn France (post French Revolution) and presented its own remarkable sphere of circumstances, notwithstanding the bold statement made by a woman of her times. Is it possible that contradictions arose within the pages as she wrote Frankenstein after reaching the inner sanctum (her goal) of Mount Blanc? Is it possible that after making these two trips she discovered something unknown, something deep within her own mind?

Mary writes:
"Even broken in spirit as he is, no one can feel more deeply than he does the beauties of nature. The starry sky, the sea, and every sight afforded by these wonderful regions seem still to have the power of elevating his soul from earth. Such a man has a double existence: he may suffer misery and be overwhelmed by disappointments, yet when he has retired into himself, he will be like a celestial spirit that has a halo around him, within whose circle no grief or folly ventures."(Frankenstein, Letter 1).

Perhaps she had been stirred from childhood passions cultivated in books written by the alchemists with the same name "Victor". Consequently, it resulted in an unrequited "ardour", to be fulfilled only by actions as she became an adult. She passed her thoughts along to her own protagonist: Victor Frankenstein. Mary's Victor leaves behind his past (alchemy), as suggested by his professors in order to join the 'new era' of natural philosophy upheld by experimentation and instruments with concrete results. Victor Frankenstein's ambition would even surpass the experiments proposed by his professors, in essence crossing the line from inanimate (dead matter) to animate (living matter), making him a first pseudo-creator.

Essentially, Mary's Frankenstein delivers us a "being" of artificial intelligence (AI). Mary constructs this storyline (unreal) based on half-truths of the time and propels us into the seemingly absurd (pseudo-reality) as an event horizon at the edge of a black hole. Although electricity was the messenger, Mary is clear in that the switch was lifted with a human hand, and was no accident. The new science of electric power completed man's goal that began in curiosity and sparked "an enthusiasm which elevates...to heaven" when realized.

Mary writes:
"These reflections have dispelled the agitation with which I began my letter, and I feel my heart glow with an enthusiasm which elevates me to heaven, for nothing contributes so much to tranquillise the mind as a steady purpose—a point on which the soul may fix its intellectual eye. This expedition has been the favourite dream of my early years. I have read with ardour the accounts of the various voyages which have been made in the prospect of arriving at the North Pacific Ocean through the seas which surround the pole." (Frankenstein, Letter 1).

In one of the final chapters of Frankenstein, Mary returns to the theme of voyages and great noble motivations as the corruption of the mind for the "daemon", and on par with "Don Quixote", which criticized "knightly" behaviour after his obsession of reading books (imagination) and his adventure (animate) to discover the falsehoods of society in real-time.

"Why does man boast of sensibilities superior to those apparent in the brute; it only renders them more necessary beings. If our impulses were confined to hunger, thirst, and desire, we might be nearly free; but now we are moved by every wind that blows and a chance word or scene that that word may convey to us." (Frankenstein, Chapter 9).

As described in her diary, Mary, like Don Quixote, delights in a picnic in a meadow; however, her character Dr Frankenstein moves humanity into the unknown territory of science fiction. She admits to the charismatic stature of Mount Blanc that stands as a pillar of literary inspirations for writers contemplating the scene from their windows, but it is her own voyage to the centre of the Alps that raises more questions of "undiscovered solitudes" that a satisfied conventional traveller just home from a vacation probably would not explore. Did the visceral experiences of the voyage stir in her a fantastical imagination, or ignite an electric shock to her synapses that opened the chasms of her mind to warn us for the future? Was her ambition satisfied, or did it leave her wanton of further voyages?

Mary adds a fragment of Pierce Shelley's poem:

"We rest; a dream has power to poison sleep.
We rise; one wand'ring thought pollutes the day.
We feel, conceive, or reason; laugh or weep,
Embrace fond woe, or cast our cares away;
It is the same: for, be it joy or sorrow,
The path of its departure still is free.
Man's yesterday may ne'er be like his morrow;
Nought may endure but mutability!"

Note: Frankenstein was not a trilogy meant to drag us into a whirlpool of "daemon"- created worlds. It was a warning. Maybe we missed her point, or maybe not? Is it too late? Her novel ends with the "daemon" escaping over the ice. Supposedly, the original protagonist (storyteller) was being passed the baton from Victor Frankenstein, noting his failed attempt. As his last dying wish, Victor warns the storyteller to pursue the "daemon", but not to be fooled by its charismatic charm of artificial intelligence.

17

My Compelling Quest

Enchanting Sanctuary (Voyage)

Interestingly enough, Mont Blanc had never been one of my travel destinations, but after reading the opening chapter of Frankenstein, which was set on the ice and snow, I found myself reviewing my own travel plans to distant lands. I recalled a daring adventure that took me to the heart of the Himalayan mountains at the base of three peaks, referred to as the "Sanctuary", situated under the sacred Annapurna Peak.

At first it seemed to be the easiest route in the valley, and quite short in comparison to the three-week routes around the outer ring of the mountains. I was accompanied by some older friends, and so the pace was easy and the trail well marked. In fact, it was a path from village to village that local kids were doing in flip flops! It was my first "trekking" experience. I had only known hiking in California, so this was a new way for me to explore the mystical mountain range. I had been only slightly prepared, with a down jacket from China and a rented sleeping bag from Kathmandu. My shoes were worn out sneakers, but we were assured that it was not a difficult trail. It would take approximately 8 days up and back. Each day we saw the mountain range in the distance, and then fog rolled in by afternoon; however, each morning provided a closer view of the mountain range that was becoming more and more spectacular. One night, in the rather rough lodging house where we stayed towards the end of the valley, travellers told us that it was almost impossible to finish the trail due to an avalanche that had covered the trail. On top of that news, it was reported that the avalanche was slipping and melting day by day.

Although it was not advised to continue, there were some young travellers who were planning on crossing the avalanche in the morning before it was drenched in sunshine and slippery with movements from melting. The day before I had met a Japanese expedition that was leaving the next morning with their professional team and base camp entourage. I spoke Japanese, and inquired if I could join them. I was set on finishing my goal! How lucky to have met this group, I thought. My initial travelling companions decided to return to Pokhara down the valley with the guide, and I joined the Japanese expedition. I gave up my pack to my companion and only took a small day pack with my sleeping bag slung over my shoulder with my jacket. The expedition had one woman (a kindergarten teacher) and I could share a tent with her. Perfect! All was set for the next morning. I waved goodbye and told my friends that I would see them in a few days. We took up the trail, and the woman was the first one out in front of the guys. These were expert climbers that had already done Mt. Everest the year before, so I felt like I was in good hands. We approached the avalanche slowly. I walked between the line of climbers with a rope and ski pole (borrowed). I just had to concentrate on looking at the feet in front of mine. I did not look up or down. As soon as we crossed, I was relieved, and thought about how relatively easy it had been following behind the experts.

We arrived to the sanctuary that afternoon before sunset. It was as magical as I had imagined. The Japanese group set up their base camp and played Kitaro music from a cassette player that they had brought along. They would be there in the base camp all season (autumn). It was their goal to climb Annapurna in winter; indeed, it had never been done before. I, however, could not imagine staying all winter. The base camp was special, with hearty food and music. I explored the next day on my own around the area that was not too extensive, but massively impressive, with three Himalayan peaks seen from every direction at 12,000 feet (4,000 m) looking up to 24,000-foot peaks (12,000 m). I stayed one more night and prepared to leave the following day. I had travelled alone at times in my life, so going down the mountain trail with villagers did not seem dangerous to me. What had not occurred to me was the return crossing of the avalanche. ALONE! Funny how when you are young you forget some important details in the risk management of life! I waved goodbye to my Japanese companions and set out, happy -go -lucky. I wanted to get a good start before dark.

Suddenly, as I was approaching the avalanche, it dawned on me...I had to cross it again by myself. I stopped at the edge. This time I looked up and down. Across from the avalanche was a cave with a makeshift tea stop where I saw local Nepalese watching me. Days before there had barely been any footprints, and it was starkly white with a clear line to follow. Now I was observing foot prints everywhere and no clear path to follow. In fact, it was dusty and confusing. I stared directly into the eyes of the Nepalese across the way in the cave and started a slow tip-toe across the slippery slush. I could not even think. It was just one foot in front of the other while holding my breath. The young Nepalese boys in the rock cave watched me, and I kept my eye on their chai cups. I do not know how I managed to cross the avalanche without panicking. As I arrived, I was greeted with smiles and a hot cup of chai.

Soon I was off to my next stop for the night. After that I began to contemplate the actual task at hand. I was trekking down the mountain alone, a woman in an unknown territory. Suddenly from behind me came some friendly voices. Two guys from Scotland were laughing away down the trail. I asked if I could join them until we came to the next village or hut. Lodgings were scarce beyond the timber line and what we found was a shack that a local man had put together with a mud floor in the side of the mountain. The great part was that he served a hot breakfast! We all agreed to stay and settled in for the night.

At dinner, I asked our host why he carried a rifle. He told us about the tigers and snakes that were all around; more frivolous oversights on my part! The person at the outpost at the bottom of the river had only given us a flimsy piece of paper with some rudimentary trail lines to follow, and NO warnings of dangers were posted. The Scottish guys asked me, "Do you do a lot of trekking?" "Me? It's my first time." They laughed, and me, too. I was beginning to understand my voyage in retrospect. In hindsight, I am not sure I would have gone to the Sanctuary if I had known all the details, but the magical mystery of the voyage propelled me forward, like Mary Shelley in her quest to the heart of the Alps. I had been watching those Himalayan peaks since I had arrived in Kathmandu and NOTHING was going to stop me from my dream in Shangri-La. It had been those stories in my imagination that had whirled me into the event horizon of an avalanche on the highest mountains in the globe!

Back on the rocks at Mont Blanc, the sounds of "crack" that locals explain as signalling an avalanche in the distant, were very near to my heart.

18

Mary's Friendships

Friendship/Equality

Mary was the daughter of a feminist (Mary Wollstonecraft) and wife of a poet (Pierce Shelley). Perhaps she longed for more female friends in the midst of her travels to share thoughts and reflections. Her marriage seemed to be of the kind of 'friendship' that her mother had written about with vigour, for young women to aspire to create a balanced world.

Mary Wollstonecraft, Sr. (mother) is described as the following:

"Women had to be educated; their minds and bodies had to be trained. This would make them good companions, wives, mothers and citizens (Brace 2000). In Wollstonecraft's view, marriages ought to have friendship rather than physical attraction as their basis (Kendrick: 2019)."

Unfortunately, Mary's mother died after childbirth from complications of surgery. Even though she had been warned of surgeons encroaching in on the profession of midwives, ironically her child (Mary) was delivered by a surgeon. Young Mary would grow up without her mother nearby, but the legacy had been firmly planted in literary texts and followed up with her father's memoirs of her mother's life.

In a diary of her own literary style with History of Six Week Tour, Mary S. Wollstonecraft distinguishes between shared memories with her husband and her solo reflections, with pronouns such as "we" and "I" to describe inner thoughts and joint discussions. From the beginning of the travel diary, it appears plans were discussed together before reaching a resolution that was pleasing to all.

*"After talking over and rejecting many plans, we fixed on one eccentric enough, but which, from its romance, was very pleasing to us. In England we could not have put it in execution without sustaining continual insult and impertinence: the French are far more tolerant of the vagaries of their neighbours. We resolved to walk through France; but as I was too weak for any considerable distance, and my sister could not be supposed to be able to walk as far as S*** [Pierce Shelley] each day, we determined to purchase an ass, to carry our portmanteau and one of us by turns." (History of Six Week Tour, p. 13)*

Actually, Pierce S. sprained his ankle early in the trip and he rode a donkey which was supposed to service the sisters. Suddenly, it was no longer women keeping up with the males by foot, but rather ensuring the comfort of an injured male in order not to abandon the expedition all together. To continue their adventure a mule driver with a carriage to carry all was sought, possibly not contemplated at first for economic reasons. It is noteworthy to observe that M. S. Wollstonecraft mentions several times their financial support was a result of her husband's business. However, their 'friendship' is noted in her writings on quite a lot of occasions throughout the diary.

"At about one we arrived at Gros Bois, where, under the shade of trees, we ate our bread and fruit, and drank our wine, thinking of Don Quixote and Sancho." (History of Six Weeks Tour, p. 16)
"The Swiss appeared to us then, and experience has confirmed our opinion, a people slow of comprehension and of action; but habit has made them unfit for slavery..." (History of Six Weeks Tour, p. 50)
"...this lovely lake, these sublime mountains, and wild forests, seemed a

fit cradle for a mind aspiring to high adventure and heroic deeds. "Such were our reflections, and we remained until late in the evening on the shores of the lake conversing, enjoying the rising breeze, and contemplating with feelings of exquisite delight the divine objects that surrounded us." (History of Six Weeks, p. 50)

"And remember this was all one scene, it all pressed home to our regard and our imagination. Though it embraced a vast extent of space, the snowy pyramids which shot into the bright blue sky seemed to overhang our path." (History of Six Weeks Tour, p. 152)

"...all was as much our own, as if we had been the creators of such impressions in the minds of others as now occupied our own." (History of Six Weeks Tour, p. 152)

Mary is clear when she writes of her own reflections and omits the 'our' or 'we' in the diary entry. Her descriptions of exceptional experiences that moved her deeply came from observations of people, cultural habits, and historical monuments or lack thereof. These notes became an integral part of her final storyline in Frankenstein to build her characters.

"...but one little boy had such exquisite grace in his mien and motions, as I never before saw equalled in a child. His countenance was beautiful for the expression with which it overflowed. There was a mixture of pride and gentleness in his eyes and lips, the indications of sensibility, which his education will probably pervert to misery or seduce to crime; but there was more of gentleness than of pride, and it seemed that the pride was tamed from its original wildness by the habitual exercise of milder feelings." (History of Six Week Tour, p. 110)

"I knew before, that if avarice could harden the hearts of men, a system of prescriptive religion has an influence far more inimical to natural sensibility. I know that an isolated man is sometimes restrained by shame from outraging the venerable feelings arising out of the memory of genius, which once made nature even lovelier than itself; but associated man holds it as the very sacrament of his union to forswear all delicacy, all benevolence, all remorse, all that is true, or tender, or sublime." (History of Six Weeks Tour, p. 134)

In her fictional novel, *Frankenstein,* we can appreciate her warnings of men taken over by insatiable pursuits, left to loneliness without friendship. Further to this concept of friendship in couples, Mary portrays the male characters as obsessed with females used as subjects for their fancy, tangled in jealousy, revenge, and/or domination---fathers choosing marriage partners. She attempts to solve these inequalities and faults of the male protagonists with storytelling mechanisms of ideals coined "noble". Nevertheless, she is describing the 'evolved' man, and yet the women in her story are left to the background. Perhaps it was her message to men, not women, that was her intent. Although she was encouraged by her husband and friends to write, she relates that her time was consumed by family duties. It was not until she was in the company of Lord Byron as a guest that she was 'free' to write. I suppose it was the reason for her finishing the base of her tale (*Frankenstein*) in a night, and relaying it to others in the morning. It was only then during that gloomy summer confined to the Byron's abode that she could work on it as her primary literary goal. She drew on her recent travels to the deep recesses of Mont Blanc where she had witnessed human relationships pushed to the brink, her own body fatigued, and all in the midst of the forces of Nature.

Friendship in Frankenstein: Two Perspectives

The story that Mary has relayed is told in three dimensions with two perspectives. There is the Dr Frankenstein version as retold in a flashback to the protagonist through four letters at the beginning of the novel. Later, there is the same story told through the eyes of the 'daemon', or 'being', created by Dr Frankenstein. The three dimensions are human, non-human (mind? artificial intelligence?) and Nature. Nature is the backdrop that contributes to the forces of the other beings as they are impacted by extreme environments with sublime and visceral experiences.

Storyteller Desire for Friendship:

"But I have one want which I have never yet been able to satisfy, and the absence of the object of which I now feel as a most severe evil, I have no friend, Margaret: when I am glowing with the enthusiasm of success, there will be none to participate my joy; if I am assailed by disappointment, no one will endeavour to sustain me in dejection. I shall commit my thoughts to paper, it is true; but that is a poor medium for the communication of feeling. I desire the company of a man who could sympathise with me, whose eyes would reply to mine. You may deem me romantic, my dear sister, but I bitterly feel the want of a friend. I have no one near me, gentle yet courageous, possessed of a cultivated as well as of a capacious mind, whose tastes are like my own, to approve or amend my plans. How would such a friend repair the faults of your poor brother!" (Frankenstein, Letter 2)

"Well, these are useless complaints; I shall certainly find no friend on the wide ocean, nor even here in Archangel, among merchants and seamen. Yet some feelings, unallied to the dross of human nature, beat even in these rugged bosoms. My lieutenant, for instance, is a man of wonderful courage and enterprise; he is madly desirous of glory, or rather, to word my phrase more characteristically, of advancement in his profession. He is an Englishman, and in the midst of national and professional prejudices, unsoftened by cultivation, retains some of the noblest endowments of humanity. I first became acquainted with him on board a whale vessel; finding that he was unemployed in this city, I easily engaged him to assist in my enterprise." (Frankenstein, Letter 2)

"The master is a person of an excellent disposition and is remarkable in the ship for his gentleness and the mildness of his discipline. This circumstance, added to his well-known integrity and dauntless courage, made me very desirous to engage him. A youth passed in solitude, my best years spent under your gentle and feminine fosterage, has so refined the groundwork of my character that I cannot overcome an intense distaste to the usual brutality exercised on board ship: I have never believed it to be necessary, and when I heard of a mariner equally noted for his kindliness of heart and the respect and obedience *paid to him by his crew, I felt myself peculiarly fortunate in being able to secure his services. I heard of him first in rather a romantic manner, from a lady who owes to him the happiness of her life."* (Frankenstein, Letter 2)

"This, briefly, is his story. Some years ago he loved a young Russian lady of moderate fortune, and having amassed a considerable sum in prize-money, the father of the girl consented to the match. He saw his mistress once before the destined ceremony; but she was bathed in tears, and throwing herself at his feet, entreated him to spare her, confessing at the same time that she loved another, but that he was poor, and that her father would never consent to the union." (Frankenstein, Letter 2)

"My generous friend reassured the suppliant, and on being informed of the name of her lover, instantly abandoned his pursuit. He had already bought a farm with his money, on which he had designed to pass the remainder of his life; but he bestowed the whole on his rival, together with the remains of his prize-money to purchase stock, and then himself solicited the young woman's father to consent to her marriage with her lover." (Frankenstein, Letter 2)

"But the old man decidedly refused, thinking himself bound in honour to my friend, who, when he found the father inexorable, quitted his country, nor returned until he heard that his former mistress was married according to her inclinations. "What a noble fellow!" you will exclaim. He is so; but then he is wholly uneducated: he is as silent as a Turk, and a kind of ignorant carelessness attends him, which, while it renders his conduct the more astonishing, detracts from the interest and sympathy which otherwise he would command." (Frankenstein, Letter 2)

"I said in one of my letters, my dear Margaret, that I should find no friend on the wide ocean; yet I have found a man who, before his spirit had been broken by misery, I should have been happy to have possessed as the brother of my heart." (Frankenstein, Letter 4)

"My affection for my guest increases every day. He excites at once my admiration and my pity to an astonishing degree. How can I see so noble a creature destroyed by misery without feeling the most poignant grief? He is so gentle, yet so wise; his mind is so cultivated, and when he speaks, although

his words are culled with the choicest art, yet they flow with rapidity and unparalleled eloquence." (Frankenstein, *Letter 4*)

He entered attentively into all my arguments in favour of my eventual success and into every minute detail of the measures I had taken to secure it. I was easily led by the sympathy which he evinced to use the language of my heart, to give utterance to the burning ardour of my soul and to say, with all the fervour that warmed me, how gladly I would sacrifice my fortune, my existence, my every hope, to the furtherance of my enterprise. One man's life or death were but a small price to pay for the acquirement of the knowledge which I sought, for the dominion I should acquire and transmit over the elemental foes of our race.

As I spoke, a dark gloom spread over my listener's countenance. At first I perceived that he tried to suppress his emotion; he placed his hands before his eyes, and my voice quivered and failed me as I beheld tears trickle fast from between his fingers; a groan burst from his heaving breast. I paused; at length he spoke, in broken accents: "Unhappy man! Do you share my madness? Have you drunk also of the intoxicating draught? Hear me; let me reveal my tale, and you will dash the cup from your lips!" (Frankenstein, *Letter 4*)

"*Having conquered the violence of his feelings, he appeared to despise himself for being the slave of passion; and quelling the dark tyranny of despair, he led me again to converse concerning myself personally. He asked me the history of my earlier years. The tale was quickly told, but it awakened various trains of reflection. I spoke of my desire of finding a friend, of my thirst for a more intimate sympathy with a fellow mind than had ever fallen to my lot, and expressed my conviction that a man could boast of little happiness who did not enjoy this blessing.* (Frankenstein, *Letter 4*)

"*I agree with you,*" *replied the stranger; "we are unfashioned creatures, but half made up, if one wiser, better, dearer than ourselves—such a friend ought to be—do not lend his aid to perfectionate our weak and faulty natures. I once had a friend, the most noble of human creatures, and am entitled, therefore, to judge respecting friendship. You have hope, and the world before you, and have no cause for despair. But I—I have lost everything and cannot begin life anew.*" (Frankenstein, *Letter 4*)

"Yesterday the stranger said to me, "You may easily perceive, Captain Walton, that I have suffered great and unparalleled misfortunes. I had determined at one time that the memory of these evils should die with me, but you have won me to alter my determination. You seek for knowledge and wisdom, as I once did; and I ardently hope that the gratification of your wishes may not be a serpent to sting you, as mine has been." (Frankenstein, Letter 4)

"I do not know that the relation of my disasters will be useful to you; yet, when I reflect that you are pursuing the same course, exposing yourself to the same dangers which have rendered me what I am, I imagine that you may deduce an apt moral from my tale, one that may direct you if you succeed in your undertaking and console you in case of failure." (Frankenstein, Letter 4)

"Prepare to hear of occurrences which are usually deemed marvellous. Were we among the tamer scenes of nature I might fear to encounter your unbelief, perhaps your ridicule; but many things will appear possible in these wild and mysterious regions which would provoke the laughter of those unacquainted with the ever-varied powers of nature; nor can I doubt but that my tale conveys in its series internal evidence of the truth of the events of which it is composed." (Frankenstein, Letter 4)

"I thank you," he replied, "for your sympathy, but it is useless; my fate is nearly fulfilled. I wait but for one event, and then I shall repose in peace. I understand your feeling," continued he, perceiving that I wished to interrupt him; "but you are mistaken, my friend, if thus you will allow me to name you; nothing can alter my destiny; listen to my history, and you will perceive how irrevocably it is determined." (Frankenstein, Letter 4)

He then told me that he would commence his narrative the next day when I should be at leisure. Even now, as I commence my task, his full-toned voice swells in my ears; his

lustrous eyes dwell on me with all their melancholy sweetness; I see his thin hand raised in animation, while the lineaments of his face are irradiated by the soul within. Strange and harrowing must be his story, frightful the storm which embraced the gallant vessel on its course and wrecked it—thus!" (Frankenstein, Letter 4)

Daemon Desire for Friendship:

"Cursed, cursed creator! Why did I live? Why, in that instant, did I not extinguish the spark of existence which you had so wantonly bestowed? I know not; despair had not yet taken possession of me; my feelings were those of rage and revenge. I could with pleasure have destroyed the cottage and its inhabitants and have glutted myself with their shrieks and misery. (Frankenstein, Chapter 16)

"When night came I quitted my retreat and wandered in the wood; and now, no longer restrained by the fear of discovery, I gave vent to my anguish in fearful howlings. I was like a wild beast that had broken the toils, destroying the objects that obstructed me and ranging through the wood with a stag-like swiftness. Oh! What a miserable night I passed! The cold stars shone in mockery, and the bare trees waved their branches above me; now and then the sweet voice of a bird burst forth amidst the universal stillness. All, save I, were at rest or in enjoyment; I, like the arch-fiend, bore a hell within me, and finding myself unsympathised with, wished to tear up the trees, spread havoc and destruction around me, and then to have sat down and enjoyed the ruin." (Frankenstein, Chapter 16)

"Another circumstance strengthened and confirmed these feelings. Soon after my arrival in the hovel I discovered some papers in the pocket of the dress which I had taken from your laboratory. At first I had neglected them, but now that I was able to decipher the characters in which they were written, I began to study them with diligence. It was your journal of the four months that preceded my creation." (Frankenstein, Chapter 16)

"You doubtless recollect these papers. Here they are. Everything is related in them which bears reference to my accursed origin; the whole detail of that series of disgusting circumstances which produced it is set in view; the minutest description of my odious and loathsome person is given, in language which painted your own horrors and rendered mine indelible. I sickened as I read. 'Hateful day when I received life!' I exclaimed in agony. 'Accursed creator! Why did you form a monster so hideous that even you turned from me in disgust?'" (Frankenstein, Chapter 16)

"God, in pity, made man beautiful and alluring, after his own image; but *my form is a filthy type of yours, more horrid even from the very resemblance. Satan had his companions, fellow devils, to admire and encourage him, but I am solitary and abhorred." (Frankenstein, Chapter 16)*

""I endeavoured to crush these fears and to fortify myself for the trial which in a few months I resolved to undergo; and sometimes I allowed my thoughts, unchecked by reason, to ramble in the fields of Paradise, and dared to fancy amiable and lovely creatures sympathising with my feelings and cheering my gloom; their angelic countenances breathed smiles of consolation. But it was all a dream; no Eve soothed my sorrows nor shared my thoughts; I was alone. I remembered Adam's supplication to his Creator. But where was mine? He had abandoned me, and in the bitterness of my heart I cursed him." (Frankenstein, Chapter 16)

"You must create a female for me with whom I can live in the interchange of those sympathies necessary for my being. This you alone can do, and I demand it of you as a right which you must not refuse to concede." (Frankenstein, Chapter 17)

"You, my creator, would tear me to pieces and triumph; remember that, and tell me why I should pity man more than he pities me? You would not call it murder if you could precipitate me into one of those ice-rifts and destroy my frame, the work of your own hands. Shall I respect man when he condemns me? Let him live with me in the interchange of kindness, and instead of injury I would bestow every benefit upon him with tears of gratitude at his acceptance. But that cannot be; the human senses are insurmountable barriers to our union. Yet mine shall not be the submission of abject slavery." (Frankenstein, Chapter 17)

"I will revenge my injuries; if I cannot inspire love, I will cause fear, and chiefly towards you my arch-enemy, because my creator, do I swear in-extinguishable hatred. Have a care; I will work at your destruction, nor finish until I desolate your heart, so that you shall curse the hour of your birth." (Frankenstein, Chapter 17)

"What I ask of you is reasonable and moderate; I demand a creature of another sex, but as hideous as myself; the gratification is small, but it is all that I can receive, and it shall content me. It is true, we shall be monsters, cut off from all the world; but on that account we shall be more attached to one

another. Our lives will not be happy, but they will be harmless and free from the misery I now feel. Oh! My creator, make me happy; let me feel gratitude towards you for one benefit! Let me see that I excite the sympathy of some existing thing; do not deny me my request!" (Frankenstein, Chapter 17).

"My food is not that of man; I do not destroy the lamb and the kid to glut my appetite; acorns and berries afford me sufficient nourishment. My companion will be of the same nature as myself and will be content with the same fare. We shall make our bed of dried leaves; the sun will shine on us as on man and will ripen our food. The picture I present to you is peaceful and human, and you must feel that you could deny it only in the wantonness of power and cruelty. Pitiless as you have been towards me, I now see compassion in your eyes; let me seize the favourable moment and persuade you to promise what I so ardently desire." (Frankenstein, Chapter 17)

Tomaselli, Sylvana, (2020). "Mary Wollstonecraft" in The Stanford Encyclopedia of Philosophy (Winter 2020 Edition), Edward N. Zalta (ed.). "When Wollstonecraft came to write *The Vindication of the Rights of Woman*, which she did within a matter of months following the publication of her first overtly political work, the moral rejuvenation of society and the happiness of individual women were woven together. It argues that women should be taught skills so as to be able to support themselves and their children in widowhood, and never have to marry or remarry out of financial necessity. It seeks to reclaim midwifery for women, against the encroachment of men into this profession, and contends that women could be physicians just as well as nurses. It urges women to extend their interests to encompass politics and the concerns of the whole of humanity. In Wollstonecraft's view, marriages ought to have friendship rather than physical attraction as their basis Kendrick (2019)."

19

My Friendships

My Friendships 2019/2020

At this moment, in January, 2021, during the aftermath of the 2nd wave of the Corona-19 virus, we are now beginning the 3rd wave, and travel has been significantly restricted since the onset of the corona virus pandemic. Unlike the past when friendships were maintained through postcards and handwritten letters, after the 19th century friends began to meet face to face, many times through travel across borders, as air travel became more and more accessible. These encounters became more frequent, to the point that travel became so easy that we began to fill up the skies with excessive air traffic; everybody was travelling! Suddenly, it halted with the onset of the pandemic in March 2020. Our friendships become virtual even if someone lived just one hour away by commuter train. We were confined to our homes, and at one point were even unable to socialize with neighbours across the hall. We lived with masks, no hugs and no kisses for greetings. Interactions became rather cold and we learned to find new ways to connect.

One of the most remarkable aspects of my friendships was the obvious bonds that had been made over our lifetimes. The level of support amongst my "tribe" was truly amazing, especially when I was living with the virus in isolation alone at home in March 2020. The daily check-in text messages continued for months during the spring of 2020 until summer. Then, as soon as the sun was shining bright with longer days, it seemed everyone wanted to travel a bit to release the built-up tension. Notwithstanding, precautions were taken to socialize as little as possible and if we did meet, to do it outdoors. I wish I had taken advantage of that period to socialize more, but I was busy planting a local organic garden. Now in winter with nothing to do in the garden, we are confined again in my town due to high levels of the unending Covid-19/20/21, not to mention the worst winter in 100 years that brought a snow storm like an artic polar express. It gave us an additional reason to be on alert to shelter in place: to avoid falling trees, icy sidewalks, and blocks of snow crashing down from sliding off rooftops.

During that Spring of 2020, my face-to-face friendships were virtually nil. I could only rely on my tiny plants for companionship. On my back porch, with the southern sun, they thrived as the days got longer and longer. I woke up to them, watered them, watched them sprout up and bid them goodnight. It was a sweet relationship with loads of rewards. This relationship was later transferred to my garden. I rode my bicycle every day in the early morning hours, passing farmers and making new friends. I learned from their stories of how to tend my garden and harvest just at the right time for the best flavours. From their advice I was lucky to end up with an abundant summer crop harvest, and our friendships carried over into the next season to help me collect my notes for the next cycle.

Meanwhile, old friendships and family encounters moved along to the next level of digital technology, with virtual meetings in group rooms and intimate chats via videos. Global summer camps, poetry readings, and even painting classes offered a refreshing ensemble of intersections to make new virtual friendships. However, the digital aspect become overwhelming, and fatigue set in with the exasperating possibilities to fit everything into a 24-hour schedule, not to mention the tunnel vision damage (physical and mental).

Finally, there was an unexpected friendship that took me by surprise: self-reflection. Me, myself and I had hours of time alone that led to opportunities of contemplation. In the beginning, I sat at my windows watching Spring outside, while inside my soul was searching for answers. Meditation took on a whole new aspect, and it seemed to be happening at odd hours. I suppose the mind has its own rudder on the turbulent seas of life. During 2020, this unique year, we were all on the same voyage, sharing a boat with no rudder. We were paddling with homemade oars upstream against a water current that came with wave after wave of commotion. No one was writing to friends and family about a rare adventure. It was a collective experience with personal memoirs that transformed us from the inside out. We were dealing with a world health crisis and a political power shift on the verge of a breakdown. We were constantly keeping our minds focused inward and outward like a teetertotter delicately balanced with two weights pushing and pulling our attention.

I was reminded of a sail boat trip I had taken on the South China Sea with two companions; an experienced sea captain and an ignorant fellow traveller. We faced the possibility of a human disaster (tyrant pirates) or natural disaster (storms). My shift at the helm was from late night to sunrise, and I would alternate my gaze from outward to inward. I scanned the dark waters, attentive to movements of pirates on the horizon. At the same time, I had to focus on the compass to keep the rudder on course. The waves were turbulent at times and I never knew how the night would end. Many times, I was greeted at sunrise by dolphins. This lasted for 11 days, with no land in sight. We arrived safely to our destination, only to hear vivid stories upon arrival of close encounters with pirates; on the other hand, we only had to deal with a storm that tore off a line of a sail, almost losing our captain in the dark waters. All those nights at the helm, I had deep reflections with the stars, and by morning I was renewed again and again.

By 2021, I found myself isolating again under the stars for a different reason. It was a coping mechanism to balance my mind to keep from falling into dark waters. I had to hold my helm steady on course to avoid thoughts of gloom. I wrote poetry and re-read Frankenstein with different eyes and ears. I found Mary's "daemon" to be part of

Dr Frankenstein's mind that had been left unchecked. By the time he had realized the mistake it was too late. He had already created the "monster", and it was no friend. His only reprieve was to ignore the charismatic voice of 'reason' that his created 'being' used to seduce him. I suppose he was fighting with his own mind. He had already lost his real friends and loved ones to the 'monster'. He sailed out into a lake in the dark night to rid himself of the parts of a female counterpart he had begun to create for his 'monster'. Now, with all the disturbing news, I found myself entrenched in a downward spiral, so I decided to step back and to be a "good" friend to myself. With discipline I refrained from any negative thoughts. I began to rid myself of these thoughts and merely 'observe' the global situation as a theatre play of actors. I stayed informed but kept myself free from the visceral effect, by keeping my mind in check. I had to side step the charismatic charm of 'reason' portrayed in the news to remain distanced from the storm, but alert.

I become my own best friend. I no longer turned to friends for solace. I went back to my plants to calm my mind. Even though it was winter, I found flowers that kept blooming on the back porch. They were frost resistant and held up through the long winter months. Every day they greeted me with their vibrant colours and healthy aspect. I retreated to a small space of meditation in my mind and reminded myself that apparent gloom would pass like the clouds (St Teresa's proverb). Outside my window the earth was full of fresh snow and sunshine. I began to focus on the 'sunbow' that appeared suddenly in the distance. I was learning this new way to describe the phenomenon that comes after a storm, based on the SUN, not the rain.

Thank you, Mary, my new literary friend, indeed.

You have taught me this alternate version of the rainbow:

"SUNBOW"

20

The Lovers of the Pinnacles

I.

B'neath
the dome
of cathedral arches,
vaulted upward
One Heart
between *Them,*
Shelley & Shelley
Sailing seas, and rivers, even
Restless rudders on wavy lakes,
Passing over bursting streams, rocky gorges,
Cascading waterfalls, sprayed with freshness
Awakening their Souls, anointing them
On a voyage, they called,
The Six weeks' Tour.

II.

Plodding-plotting
'round
Her temple, the Alps,
destiny Divine
Soaking up meadow melodies,
insect chatter, honeycombs
They blended well in shade of trees,
like young seedlings,
restoring ancient woods,
Swayed by wildflowers, rare unseen,
unknown palette, standing ground,
akin to Julie & Saint-Preux
Fortified their *Love*,
As man & wife,
A friendship moulded
of vernal poets, poetic verse,
Uni-verse, they wrote.

III.

Under one sky, behold
their pens, whilst dreaming
more than one an-other,
none-the-less (nonetheless)
Apart, together, in unison.
Nature drew them into Her
a spell cast long before
On the threshold
Of human vice
Enticed---
"explore!"
beyond your
native
land.

IV.

Their hearts
bare testimony---
As they submerge together.
Neptune thrusts *himself*
from below, breaking free
from obscurity,
Aurora longs to reveal *herself*
from above, unconfined,
from captivity.

V.

Clouds split open,
Confessions roar,
as so below, so above
naked ears,
reveal
the naked eye
Rupture
social norms---
gods and goddesses
discoverer, discovered
him Self
her Self
ONESELF

VI.

Bound
by no other, *otherness*
B' tween fe/male---male
Inner, intuition,
Outer, activation.
volcanic fire, Swirling,

churning, ocean rift
released
its charm---
pristine Earth,
is born,
anew.

VII.

While Percy Bysshe Shelley
alludes to Nature's overshadow,
Mary Shelley Wollstonecraft
exalts us forward
to recognize,
our Human shadow, mind
on the wall, itself.
Plainly Plato,
Lyrically poetic
Sung on Sapho's harp.
Nature's force sublime
between them
The Lovers
Pressed together like wildflowers
Pressed into a book,
muted colours, weathered
To Be or Not Be
at all.

VIII.

A litmus test for *our* mind
Left and right brain,
electrocuted,
shocked into a siege

A siege that bursts
through seams of *Love*
our other side
of
SELF.

IX.
Love
of Nature
Love
of Madness
Love gone, so awry.
Yet saved
between *their* pages
as a fragment, fragrant
as fresh as wildflowers plucked,
preserved, from years gone by.

X.
Of
their
imagination,
Echoing, Immobile
Under this Dome
Of stained-glass,
broken
Cathedral arches
No longer
protect
Beauty,
beholden,
I have not forgotten
Liturgy of Love

Merely
un-covered
Snow and Ice
In *Her* image
Still,
fresh
Seated, once, together
ONE throne.
Song of the Songs,

XI.

As
the *Lovers'* lines
pierce my heart today,
I admit, I sense,
new and buoyant auras
floating on the waves
Attuned to harps,
unstrung, unsung,
to fill the shadows
of the *Lovers.*

21

Mary's Nature 1819

Mary was enamoured with her surroundings of rare wildflowers (unseen in her native England) and sunbows (rainbows) on waterfalls, igniting her admiration of Nature "adorned with a thousand of the rarest flowers" and noting the "humming of sun-loving insects." She expresses the freedom she feels amongst this essence of beauty; "I feel as happy as a new-fledged bird, and hardly care what twig I fly to, so that I may try my new-found wings." Her descriptions are constantly paralleled with the Nature she encounters, "pursuing, like the swallow, the inconstant summer of delight and beauty".

It is through nature that she finds an unusual companionship to inspire her beyond her circle of 'friends'. At times she ventures out on her own to experience the landscape and immerse herself in Nature before her 'companion' wakes from sleep.* There she finds a healthy solitude sparked by daylight in her laboratory of creativeness that ignites the muse of joy.

"Those whose youth has been past as their's (with what success it imports not) in pursuing, like the swallow, the inconstant summer of delight and beauty which invests this visible world, will perhaps find some entertainment

in following the author, with her husband and sister, on foot, through part of France and Switzerland, and in sailing with her down the castled Rhine, through scenes beautiful in themselves, but which, since she visited them, a great Poet has clothed with the freshness of a diviner nature." (History of Six Weeks Tour, p. iv-v)

"As my companion rises late, I had time before breakfast, on the ensuing morning, to hunt the waterfalls of the river that fall into the lake at St. Gingoux. The stream is indeed, from the declivity over which it falls, only a succession of waterfalls, which roar over the rocks with a perpetual sound, and suspend their unceasing spray of the leaves and flowers that overhang and adorn its savage banks. The path that conducted along this river sometimes avoided the precipices of its shores, by leading through meadows; sometimes threaded the base of the perpendicular and caverned rocks. I gathered in these meadows a nosegay of such flowers as I never saw in England, and which I thought more beautiful for that rarity." (History of Six Weeks Tour, p. 126)

"To what a different scene are we now arrived! To the warm sunshine and to the humming of sun-loving insects."

"...coming to this delightful spot during this divine weather, I feel as happy as a new-fledged bird, and hardly care what twig I fly to, so that I may try my new-found wings. A more experienced bird may be more difficult in its choice of a bower; but in my present temper of mind, the budding flowers, the fresh grass of spring, and the happy creatures about me that live and enjoy these pleasures, are quite enough to afford me exquisite delight, even though clouds should shut out Mont Blanc from my sight." (History of Six Week Tour, p. 94)

"We dined there, and had some honey, the best I have ever tasted, the very essence of the mountain flowers, and as fragrant. Probably the village derives its name from this production. Mellerie is the well-known scene of St. Preux's visionary exile; but Mellerie is indeed enchanted ground, were Rousseau no magician. In the midst of these woods are dells of lawny expanse, inconceivably verdant, adorned with a thousand of the rarest flowers and odorous[sic] with thyme. (History of Six Weeks Tour, p.119).

She was aware of her responsibility as a writer and nature lover, remarking on younger trees that grow beneath the older groves, "to afford a shade to future worshippers of nature." However, all along the trail to Mont Blanc the darker side of Nature had already been revealed, with the shadows and power of the raw elements that dwarfed her in size, and realizing not even her companions could save her on the border of life and death.

"The hay was making under the trees; the trees themselves were aged, but vigorous, and interspersed with younger ones, which are destined to be their successors, and in future years, when we are dead, to afford a shade to future worshippers of nature, who love the memory of that tenderness and peace of which this was the imaginary abode." (History of Six Weeks Tour, p.131-32)

"Two leagues from Neufchatel we saw the Alps: range after range of black mountains are seen extending one before the other, and far behind all, towering above every feature of the scene, the snowy Alps. They are a hundred miles distant, but reach so high in the heavens, that they look like those accumulated clouds of dazzling white that arrange themselves on the horizon during summer. Their immensity staggers the imagination, and so far, surpasses all conception, that it requires an effort of the understanding to believe that they indeed form a part of the earth." (History of Six Weeks Tour, p.43)

"The scenery perpetually grows more wonderful and sublime: pine forests of impenetrable thickness, and untrodden, nay, inaccessible expanse spread on every side. Sometimes the dark woods descending, follow the route into the vallies [sic], the distorted trees struggling with knotted roots between the most barren clefts...". (History of Six Weeks Tour, p.89)

"The lake appeared somewhat calmer as we left Mellerie, sailing close to the banks ...the wind gradually increased in violence, until it blew tremendously...produced waves of a frightful height, and covered the whole surface with a chaos of foam...one wave fell in, and then another...and still in imminent peril from the immensity of the waves...I felt in this near prospect of death a mixture of sensations, among which terror entered..." (History of Six Weeks Tour, P. 121-22)

She moves away from the pessimistic "gloomy theory" that the ice age would return, an idea proposed by Buffon. Instead, upon hearing local storylines of glacier movements in summer and winter, she summarises that the glaciers are part of a perpetual existence as a cycle of life. She is calmed with the beauty of the ice that penetrates her heart and she embraces a humbled admiration of Nature.

"It is agreed by all, that the snow on the summit of Mont Blanc and the neighbouring mountains perpetually augments, and that ice, in the form of glaciers, subsists without melting in the valley of Chamouni during its transient and variable summer. If the snow which produces this glacier must augment, and the heat of the valley is no obstacle to the perpetual existence of such masses of ice as have already descended into it, the consequence is obvious; the glaciers must augment and will subsist, at least until they have overflowed this vale." (p. 161 History)

"I will not pursue Buffon's sublime but gloomy theory — that this globe which we inhabit will at some future period be changed into a mass of frost by the encroachments of the polar ice, and of that produced on the most elevated points of the earth." (History of Six Weeks Tour, P. 161-62)

However, with the thunder and lightning occurring in the gloomy weeks that follow her visit to Mont Blanc, in that unusual summer of no sun, she finds a pessimistic despair and fear leaking from the 'other' side of her brain. The environmental anomaly of 1816 was a seemingly perpetual cloud of dreariness (ash from Mt. Tambora) that eventually reached Mary's doorstep. It painted a rather enigmatic backdrop to create her paradoxical tale of a beauty (splendour creation) and a beast (super-human force) wrapped up in one. Her literary constructs of science fiction in relating human desires to technically overreach Nature and eventually create a destructive force beyond human containment was prophetic.

Mary admits she was always a daydreamer, but her nightmare reached inside her subconscious where uncomfortable feelings and sensations are buried with little chance of surfacing, only to become tangible elements in real-time life. However, the weather outside her window each day had no sunshine. It was not an environment for frivolous daydreamers. Mary was astonished by the thunderstorms during her second trip in 1816, as compared to her 1814 trip just prior to reaching her writing desk at Lord Byron's abode. She was a survivor of her own extraordinary tangible experiences and that phenomenon propelled her further than any other daydream. It inspired a writer that sent a warning 200 years ago. Have we been listening to her echo on this anniversary in 2019? Could we still ignore the view over yonder outside our own window that now was closer upon our own doorsteps, and even beginning to reveal itself from inside our own souls?

"Unfortunately we do not now enjoy those brilliant skies that hailed us on our first arrival to this country. An almost perpetual rain confines us principally to the house; but when the sun bursts forth it is with a splendour and heat unknown in England. The thunder storms that visit us are grander and more terrific than I have ever seen before. We watch them as they approach from the opposite side of the lake, observing the lightning play among the clouds in various parts of the heavens, and dart in jagged figures... dark with the shadow of the overhanging cloud, while perhaps the sun is shining cheerily upon us. One night we enjoyed a finer storm than I had ever before beheld. The lake was lit up...and all the scene illuminated for an instant, when a pitchy blackness succeeded, and the thunder came in frightful bursts over our heads amid the darkness." (History of Six Tour, p. 99)

"As we approached Evian, the mountains descended more precipitously to the lake, and masses of intermingled wood and rock overhung its shining spire. We arrived at this town about seven o'clock, after a day which involved more rapid changes of atmosphere than I ever recollect to have observed before. The morning was cold and wet; then an easterly wind, and the clouds hard and high; then thunder showers, and wind shifting to every quarter; then a warm blast from the south, and summer clouds hanging over the peaks, with bright blue sky between. About half an hour after we had arrived at Evian, a few flashes of lightning came from a dark cloud, directly overhead, and continued after the cloud had dispersed. " Diespiter, per pura tonantes egit equos:" [Jupiter, thanks to the pure thunder horses] a phenomenon which certainly had

*no influence on me, corresponding with that which it produced on Horace."
History of Six Weeks Tour, P. 115)*

 Shelley, M. (1817). History of a six weeks' tour, Introduction. Mary uses the term 'husband' only twice in the travel diary introduction. In the remaining pages (183 total), she uses the word 'companion'.

22

My Nature 2019

In 1819 Mary was facing theories of a return to an Ice Age, but after her visit to the glaciers at Mont Blanc, she changed her mind. Throughout her travel diary, she constantly uses the term "perpetual", and it is perhaps the most repetitive adjective in the entire literary text. Interestingly, the Navajo Nation utilizes this concept in their mission statement of their parks and recreation: "protect, preserve and manage tribal parks, monuments and recreation areas for the perpetual enjoyment..."1 Note below how Mary often times describes the essence of the waters that spring from Mont Blanc and its glaciers as the source of perpetual life!

"We went between the mountains and the lake, under groves of mighty chesnut [sic] trees, beside perpetual streams, which are nourished by the snows above, and form stalactites on the rocks, over which they fall." (History of Six Weeks' Tour, p. 123-24)

"The stream is indeed, from the declivity over which it falls, only a succession of waterfalls, which roar over the rocks with a perpetual sound, and suspend their unceasing spray on the leaves and flowers that overhang and adorn its savage banks. (History of Six Weeks' Tour, p. 126)

"The glaciers perpetually move onward, at the rate of a foot each day, with a motion that commences at the spot where on the boundaries of perpetual congelation, they are produced by the freezing of the waters which arise from the partial melting of the eternal snows." (History of Six Weeks' Tour, p. 158)

"No one dares to approach it; for the enormous pinnacles of ice which perpetually fall, are perpetually reproduced." (History of Six Weeks' Tour, p. 160)

"If the snow which produces this glacier must augment, and the heat of the valley is no obstacle to the perpetual existence of such masses of ice as have already descended into it, the consequence is obvious; the glaciers must augment and will subsist, at least until they have overflowed this vale." (History of Six Weeks' Tour, p. 161)

In 2021 we are struggling with climate changes that have been accelerated beyond comprehension and admittedly need immediate attention. The climate crisis has become a global issue that faces us as a threat of planetary extinction, under the same sky around the globe. Mary's perspective was a sense of a 'perpetual' stream of waters that nourished Europe. The volcanic eruption in Indonesia of Mt. Tambora in 1819, which created a cloud of ash that circulated the globe in the natural air stream, was certainly daunting. During that summer with no sun Mary was not aware of its consequences. She was part of its global impact, and suffered those "gloomy" days without much explanation.

I am here in January 2021 on the European continent where we have just suffered the coldest winter on the Iberian Plateau in the last 100 years! Thermometers dropped to chilling temperatures and a storm of 30 hours left behind 20 inches of snow. It has been reported as part of a polar vortex collapse.

"Losing all that ice allowed a great deal of extra heat from the sun to warm the Arctic waters, which is now being released back into the atmosphere, creating bulges of warm air in those key regions...these bulges can make northward swings in the jet stream larger, stronger, and more persistent, which in turn can disrupt the polar vortex." (National Geographic, January 2021)

My trip to Mont Blanc in 2019 depressed me after having seen the marked difference from 2015-2019 of the glacier recessions. The acceleration of this defrosting of the glaciers has been a constant reminder of Mary's view 200 years ago of "perpetual" waters of the Alps that have eroded in 2019 from infinite to finite. Unfortunately, climate change agreements from Rio to Paris since the first Earth Summit in 1992 have struggled to be signed by the global village due to market forces at play.

The urgency to save our water resources and ecosystems are the themes of lawmakers, while their beauty has been saturated by artists and walkers over time. Painters in the 19thcentury attested to the majestic glaciers reaching down to the valley that Mary saw, naturalists have confirmed their exquisiteness with their historical expeditions around Mont Blanc since 1760, all remarking about how stunned they were by its beauty and magnitude.

In the spring of 2019, it became obvious that our "perpetual" delays of climate change action in signed agreements had fallen short. Then we watched Nature take over the helm. When the pandemic of Covid-19 emerged across the planet with devastating unknown consequences, lockdowns brought the global village to a standstill, and with the significant lower human activity wildlife roamed free. Lions came out of the grasslands and slept on warm roads in plain sight (South Africa), while dolphins frolicked in city harbours amongst the stillness of boat engines (Barcelona). We shared these digital photos online from our confined shelters. The "jet" stream was on hold. We were breathing clean air again and the "air stream" began to flow with ease.

Mother Nature portrayed her beauty in an innocuous manner that sent reverberations across her domain, planet Earth. I was a witness to that beauty. As I gasped to breathe during my Covid-19 struggle with lower oxygen levels to my brain, beauty entered my soul with the melodic twill of birds singing in the morning, and drops of rain rolling down my window. I felt the tears of the Earth that could be my own tears. I merged with Nature like never before in those short weeks. As there was much less traffic during this time, I was captivated by the bird songs and their resilience. I reflected on the fact that normally these sweet melodies would have been drowned out by car noise. Hence, once the traffic began to turn to normal I missed their innocence and joy that lockdown had brought to me. I am aware that we are entering into a "new era", but it is not the one I had imagined in 1985. Rather it is a geological change caused by human activity coined "Anthropocene", after 12,000 years of steady climate since the last ice age. Believe it or not, there are disagreements on declaring the 'anthropogenic era' as a "real" geological change. Coming back to the glacier decline around the globe, however, scholars do acknowledge its existence as a human footprint "confirming a connection between anthropogenic emissions and high annual ice loss." (Vargo et al. 2020).

Mary Shelley Wollstonecraft and I experienced the glaciers, albeit 200 years apart. We both were moved by their beauty and natural force. I wonder, if she were alive today, what she would write? It is difficult to bury Frankenstein as it mutates, seeping into our consciousness. The "daemon" in our own midst lives within our own "modern" lifestyles. Is only a lockdown the way forward? Will we or the planet survive this *new* Anthropocene age?

We are no longer in a *romantic* poetic age, but rather a deafening poetic rap that is as razor sharp as those pinnacles on the edge of the last glaciers in Europe. Ironically, I can see Evian water bottled up in plastic piling up on the shores of distant beaches, quite a contrast to Mary's encounter with the village 200 years ago. The water was sacred and local then. It appears that we've lost our way on the trail back to Paris, and now it will have to be an individual responsibility to sign our own accord with Nature. I am willing to begin. You may say "I am a dreamer..." but it takes a village to heal. I am ready to dance to the beat of Nature. Back around 1992, as the Earth Summit was convening, I wrote this poetic line from a room of my own; "touch and be touched, said the drum to the drummer." It was stimulated after my first African drum lesson. I could feel the drum reverberate in my hands, showing me the next beat naturally. I am back to play in a larger drum circle. Won't you join me? I am sure we can bury Frankenstein together, and put our minds to rest.

Gountry Walkers (2020) Blog, Mont Blanc, History: "Modern mountaineering traces its roots back to 1760, when Swiss naturalist Horace Benedict de Saussure arrived in the Chamonix Valley and couldn't believe the beauty and magnitude of Mont Blanc rising above him."

Vargo, L.J., Anderson, B.M., Dadić, R. et al. (2020) Anthropogenic warming forces extreme annual glacier mass loss," in Nature Climate Change,10, 856–861. Abstract: "Here we apply event attribution methods to document this at the regional scale, targeting the highest mass-loss years (2011 and 2018) across New Zealand's Southern Alps. We estimate extreme mass loss was at least six times (2011) and ten times (2018) (>90% confidence) more likely to occur with anthropogenic forcing than without. This increased likelihood is driven by present-day temperatures ~1.0 °C above the pre-industrial average, confirming a connection between anthropogenic emissions and high annual ice loss. These results suggest that as warming and extreme heat events continue and intensify, there will be an increasingly visible human fingerprint on extreme glacier mass-loss years in the coming decades."

23

Mary's Ethics 1819

Mary's Invention: Dr. Frankenstein

In 1816, Mary, in her fullest ethical spectrum, ardently rallies between the obsessed mind of human pursuit balanced against ethical decisions. As early as Chapter 4 of *Frankenstein*, she outlines this dilemma, exploring the inner dialogue of the protagonist's mind, tempting him to forge artificial creation with electricity by human hands, void of magic or shamanistic means. It is well documented that as a young woman Mary was a witness to the rise of two schools of thought, namely 'vitalism' and 'naturalism', which were questioned by theologians. Poets like Coleridge (*Ancient Mariner) and* Wordsworth were prominent in her father's circle of thinkers as literary figures that relied on the essence of Nature to guide them in their pursuit of inner salvation. At the same time, floating around her father's house were the ideas of the scientist Sir Humphry Davy; chemistry perspectives and the advancements in electricity by means of certain metal compositions as conductors (Hogsette: 2011). In his *Elements of Chemical Philosophy* (p. 142), Davy proposed that an experiment be conducted on an animal "recently deprived of life" in which it be hooked up with two metals to its nerves and muscles , noting, "violent contractions of the limb will be occasioned." Mary Shelley was known to have read this book. Davy also pays tribute to the early scientists who contributed to the field of electricity, such as Benjamin Franklin.

The questions of scientific responsibility and ethical decisions arise in scholarly research:

"Victor Frankenstein fails in his profession because he consistently contravenes three basic tenets of scientific community: observation, repetition, and transparency. Critics of Frankenstein have generally failed to recognize the socially responsible scientific values that Shelley attempts to define through the character of the creature. Her [M. Shelley] fictional experiments with the idea of socially responsible science enable us to read Frankenstein as a work of science fiction that offers both a utopian ethic of intellectual partnership and a critique of singular science. If Shelley's vision of a more open and reflective scientific community aspired to a potentially impossible ideal, it is one toward which she thought her age should aspire" (Nicholson: 2020).

Mary outlines a dilemma for Victor Frankenstein as he contemplates, "the power placed within my hands" and becomes aware of "my ability to give life to an animal as complex and wonderful as man". Wollstonecraft gives the reader a stark gaze at the future, with the mad scientist's reasoning for sitting at the table of the wisest 'men' beyond 'magic' based on scientific theory.

Mary writes:

"when I considered the improvement which every day takes place in science and mechanics, I was encouraged to hope my present attempts would at least lay the foundations of future success." (Frankenstein, Chapter 4)

What had been the study and desire of the wisest men since the creation of the world was now within my grasp. Not that, like a magic scene, it all opened upon me at once: the information I had obtained was of a nature rather to direct my endeavours so soon as I should point them towards the object of my search than to exhibit that object already accomplished. (Frankenstein, Chapter 4)

How does Mary present the ethical decisions or lack thereof? Here the weakness attached to the pursuit of 'pure knowledge' beyond "common" sense rears its ugly head. She demonstrates that Victor, a human figure that once belonged to a community of "commoners", was encouraged to move to Ingolstadt to attend 'higher' studies, becoming Dr Frankenstein. His transformation, the male initiation, was 'normal' for lot of young boys. Although he had already begun his studies at home in the private libraries of his father and uncle, his full entry into 'manhood' would be completed with his professors' suggestions and the encouragement they gave him to overcome his predecessors.

"The possession of these treasures gave me extreme delight; I now continually studied and exercised my mind upon these histories, whilst my friends were employed in their ordinary occupations." (Frankenstein, Chapter 15)

Frustration in Victor's foreign circumstances in Ingolstadt drove him to delve deeper into a world of insatiable knowledge, with recommended readings that were considered a vital component of educating young men of his time period for ambitious goals. Wollstonecraft cleverly shows her readers the fallacies of educating youth with only a few examples, namely *Paradise Lost*, *Plutarch's Lives*, and *The Sorrows of Werter*. What is astonishing is that it is the 'daemon' that relates this concept in Mary's *Frankenstein*, as the 'monster' attempts to explain his faulty personality; blaming human literary devices as his only resource into understanding how to behave in the 'human world'.

"The volume of Plutarch's Lives which I possessed contained the histories of the first founders of the ancient republics. This book had a far different effect upon me from the Sorrows of Werter. I learned from Werter's imaginations despondency and gloom, but Plutarch taught me high thoughts; he elevated me above the wretched sphere of my own reflections, to admire and love the heroes of past ages. (Frankenstein, Chapter 15)
"Many things I read surpassed my understanding and experience. I had a very confused knowledge of kingdoms, wide extents of country, mighty rivers,

and boundless seas. But I was perfectly unacquainted with towns and large assemblages of men. The cottage of my protectors had been the only school in which I had studied human nature, but this book developed new and mightier scenes of action." (Frankenstein, Chapter 15)

"I read of men concerned in public affairs, governing or massacring their species. I felt the greatest ardour for virtue rise within me, and abhorrence for vice, as far as I understood the signification of those terms, relative as they were, as I applied them, to pleasure and pain alone. Induced by these feelings, I was of course led to admire peaceable lawgivers, Numa, Solon, and Lycurgus, in preference to Romulus and Theseus." (Frankenstein, Chapter 15)

"The patriarchal lives of my protectors caused these impressions to take a firm hold on my mind; perhaps, if my first introduction to humanity had been made by a young soldier, burning for glory and slaughter, I should have been imbued with different sensations." (Frankenstein, Chapter 15)

Further, upon its failures to 'fit into' the human world and its demonization due to its ugliness, the 'monster' attempts to reason with Victor in a "charismatic voice". The 'daemon' commands the solution to end the nightmare with an ultimatum: Dr Frankenstein must create his perfect mate, a female version of the monster. In this manner, Mary is able to reanimate Victor's ethical decision-making process as a second chance. It is based on the fear to take the easy route in creating another 'monster', or stand up to his own ethics to rid the world of *another* disastrous 'creation'. Victor acknowledges that the 'unknown' consequences on the second "creation" could prove worse. Therefore, he employs a rather unique risk management strategy to the new situation that had not existed in his mind the first time in his 'obsessed' pursuit of knowledge.

Mary Shelley was prophetic in her 'science fiction' and ethical questioning of science in its pursuit of 'pure' knowledge devoid of consequences. Perhaps we have ignored her genius. In Dr Frankenstein's second chance scenario, Mary outlines the basis of his first thoughts. It is not without feelings towards his 'creation', akin to a "mother" who cannot say 'No' to her son. Ultimately, it is fear that drove him into the creation of a female "being", to avoid the threats of the "daemon" that had made him consequently a slave. Victor had not envisioned that possibility in his first experiment. Nor had he calculated the evil doings of the 'daemon' as part of his own crime. Due to his anonymity as *creator (anonymous: abbreviation 'anon')*, Victor had not been linked to the murders of the 'daemon'. Victor tried to uphold his supposedly clean reputation and long-standing innocence with that secret. Thus, Mary pushes the reader into the next phase of ethics. Victor was resolved to continue his experiments to satisfy the "daemon", his own creation.

"I was moved. I shuddered when I thought of the possible consequences of my consent, but I felt that there was some justice in his argument. His tale and the feelings he now expressed proved him to be a creature of fine sensations, and did I not as his maker owe him all the portion of happiness that it was in my power to bestow? He saw my change of feeling and continued..." (Frankenstein, Chapter 15)

"I did not doubt but that the monster followed me and would discover himself to me when I should have finished, that he might receive his companion... With this resolution I traversed the northern highlands and fixed on one of the remotest of the Orkneys as the scene of my labours. It was a place fitted for such a work, being hardly more than a rock whose high sides were continually beaten upon by the waves. The soil was barren, scarcely affording pasture for a few miserable cows..."

"In this manner I distributed my occupations when I first arrived, but as I proceeded in my labour, it became every day more horrible and irksome to me. Sometimes I could not prevail on myself to enter my laboratory for several days, and at other times I toiled day and night in order to complete my work. It was, indeed, a filthy process in which I was engaged. During my first experiment, a kind of enthusiastic frenzy had blinded me to the horror of my employment; my mind was intently fixed on the consummation of my labour, and my eyes were shut to the horror of my proceedings. But now I went to it in cold blood, and my heart often sickened at the work of my hands." (Frankenstein, Chapter 19)

Finally, Mary's *Frankenstein* offers readers a transformation in human thought, with calculations beyond human selfishness. Wollstonecraft rips open the consciousness of a scientist to re-join the community of humans, leaving behind his ambitions. Victor envisions the possible extinction of the whole human race in its entirety with his second 'creation'. He is no longer deciding for his small circle of friends and family. Nor is he worried about how, "future ages might curse me [him] as their pest."

"Had I right, for my own benefit, to inflict this curse upon everlasting generations? I had before been moved by the sophisms of the being I had created; I had been struck senseless by his fiendish threats; but now, for the first time, the wickedness of my promise burst upon me; I shuddered to think that future ages might curse me as their pest, whose selfishness had not hesitated to buy its own peace at the price, perhaps, of the existence of the whole human race." (Frankenstein, Chapter 19)

"I left the room, and locking the door, made a solemn vow in my own heart never to resume my labours; and then, with trembling steps, I sought my own apartment. I was alone; none were near me to dissipate the gloom and relieve me from the sickening oppression of the most terrible reveries." (Frankenstein, Chapter 19)

"The night passed away, and the sun rose from the ocean; my feelings became calmer, if it may be called calmness when the violence of rage sinks into the depths of despair. I left the house, the horrid scene of the last night's contention, and walked on the beach of the sea, which I almost regarded as an insuperable barrier between me and my fellow creatures; nay, a wish that such should prove the fact stole across me." (Frankenstein, Chapter 19)

"When it became noon, and the sun rose higher, I lay down on the grass and was overpowered by a deep sleep. I had been awake the whole of the preceding night, my nerves were agitated, and my eyes inflamed by watching and misery. The sleep into which I now sank refreshed me; and when I awoke, I again felt as if I belonged to a race of human beings like myself, and I began to reflect upon what had passed with greater composure." (Frankenstein, Chapter 19)

"Nothing could be more complete than the alteration that had taken place

in my feelings since the night of the appearance of the dæmon. I had before regarded my promise with a gloomy despair as a thing that, with whatever consequences, must be fulfilled; but I now felt as if a film had been taken from before my eyes and that I for the first time saw clearly. The idea of renewing my labours did not for one instant occur to me; the threat I had heard weighed on my thoughts, but I did not reflect that a voluntary act of mine could avert it. I had resolved in my own mind that to create another like the fiend I had first made would be an act of the basest and most atrocious selfishness, and I banished from my mind every thought that could lead to a different conclusion." (Frankenstein, Chapter 19)

Mary creatively demonstrates the challenges of the mind to stay on focus with an ethical decision, as other 'rational' thoughts emerge to detract it from reality. There was an "alteration" in Victor's feelings with the reflection of daylight. It is in the sunshine that her protagonist is awakened, escaping the gloomy despair of night. Mary's ghost story was 'created' during that summer with NO sun, and was especially brave being written by a young woman. In fact, Mary published Frankenstein anonymously at first in 1818, then under her real name in 1819.

The ending of the story is in the North Pole where magnetic and electrical waves are in full force along with the colourful Aurora Borealis on display. Perhaps for the 'monster' this place provides peace and beauty near its origins of life (electricity) as it roams free. Surely, it is closer to the feet of its *mother*, Aurora, the Goddess of dawn.

<h1 style="text-align:center">2 4</h1>

My Ethics 2020

Ethic Reflections

200 years after *Frankenstein* was published in 1819, I am drawn into my own ethical decisions that I have been silently grappling with over the past few years. In writing this book, I searched for insights into the poem by Pierce Shelley that Mary inserted in Chapter 10 of *Frankenstein*; the poem speaks of her dreams, and I was especially drawn to its last lines:

It is the same: for, be it joy or sorrow,
The path of its departure still is free.
Man's yesterday may ne'er be like his morrow;
'Nought may endure but mutability!'

Strangely enough, when I searched for "Shelley and Mutability" on my web browser, I entered into a rabbit hole of scientific papers on genetic engineering. I suppose it was an algorithm that led me down the *path,* given the "cookies" embedded in my computer. I have read neurological studies on tactile perception; thus, it made some sense given my prior searches in the scientific sphere. However, I was looking for literary references to the poem. Instead, at the top of the search list I found: *"Nought May Endure but Mutability": Spliceosome Dynamics and the Regulation of Splicing* (Duncan: 2008). Curious, I reviewed the abstracts and read parts of the study, which led me down the hole deeper into the subject. One line caught my attention in the study:

"As a mutation is more likely to disrupt an interaction than to form a new one, it is likely that relative stabilization takes the form of destabilization of the competing conformation, such that most first step suppressors would destabilize the second step conformation and vice versa. At present, however, the molecular basis of the action of these general suppressor mutations is unknown." (Duncan J. Smith et al.: 2008; 660)

My next question was "What is *Spliceosome* dynamics?" I searched further, and seven pages into the article, on p. 657, I found the following:

"Assembly can be stimulated or repressed by the binding of general or specific splicing factors to snRNPs and pre-mRNA. snRNPs can also interact both with pre-mRNA and with each other. Spliceosome assembly is, thus, highly cooperative, and the fact that many interactions can occur independently of one another results in an assembly cascade that does not follow a single obligatory trajectory but instead can occur via multiple pathways." (Duncan: 2008: 657)

Through a series of studies, I educated myself on spliceosome dynamics and genetic engineering. Next, I did not understand the term 'Saccharomyces cerevisiae, noted by the study in the Duncan reference list titled: "High-density yeasttiling array reveals previously undiscovered introns and extensive regulation of meiotic splicing (Juneau, et al.: 2007). The yeast was mentioned as the best growth factor for gene discovery across species. Later, I found the study, "Screening Approaches to Identify Genes Required for DNA Double-Strand Break Damage Signaling in the Yeast Saccharomyces cerevisiae" (Bennett: 2010). Its chapter review was described as the following:

"The yeast Saccharomyces cerevisiae is at the forefront of gene discovery in a wide variety of biologic processes largely because of the relatedness between genes and function across species, the ability to utilize yeast as an in vivo test tube for genes from other species. Importantly, the availability of isogenic genome-wide deletion collections has provided ready global access to networks that impact a variety of stress responses and biological activities. This is especially evident in the numerous reports of genes identified in genome-wide screens that confer resistance to the lethal effects of a variety of DNA damaging agents that can cause DNA double strand breaks (DSBs). Moreover, combining these genome-wide screens with complete genome mRNA expression analysis can reveal details of the complex genetic circuitry required to respond to perturbations and suggest new participants in signaling pathways." (Bennett: 2010)

"This chapter provides an introduction to the approaches adopted to identify genes required for DNA double-strand break damage signaling in the yeast Saccharomyces cerevisiae...More recently, a damage sensitive mutant screening approach (DSMU) has uncovered a G1/S and S phase checkpoint adaptation defect in diploid ccr4 mutants following irradiation or replication stress induced by hydroxyurea (HU). Signaling defective mutants can be identified through secondary screens with replication mutants...The rfc4-2 mutant is lethal in combination with a mutant (rfa1-t11) of RFA1 that encodes a subunit of the DNA binding protein RPA required for G2/M adaptation." (Bennett: 2010)

I was then curious about mRNA that appeared in these studies. Believe it or not, I rounded the curve in space and found Einstein's theory of relativity on my doorstep. I was back to the beginning of my dilemma in 2019. Covid-19 vaccinations were linked to this research in 2020 via terms such as 'mRNA'. I found a quick overview of vaccines: "COVID-19 Vaccine: A comprehensive status report."

"mRNA is an emerging, non-infectious, and a non-integrating platform with almost no potential risk of insertional mutagenesis. Currently, the non-replicating RNA and the virus derived self-replicating RNAs are being studied. The immunogenicity of the mRNA can be minimized, and alterations can be

made to increase the stability of these vaccines. Furthermore, the anti-vector immunity is also avoided as the mRNA is the minimally immunogenic genetic vector, allowing repeated administration of the vaccine. This platform has empowered the rapid vaccine development program due to its flexibility and ability to mimic the antigen structure and expression as seen in the course of a natural infection." (Kaur & Gupta: 2020).

I was ready to crawl out of the rabbit hole and meander back to the literary references on the poem. How easily I was following Alice to the 'tea party' with the mad hatter at the head of the table, and the clock ticking forward and backward at the same 'time'! I admit the algorithms did in fact drive me to an unknown destination, but they seem to be based on my *own* rationale or perception of that mindset. Is this a *Frankenstein syndrome*? The challenge in 2020 is how much am I a slave to the 'cookie monster' and where do I draw the line? Has Dr Frankenstein re-emerged in modern day scientific debates? How can I bury this Frankenstein syndrome 200 years later? Can I break free from the algorithms?

I am now faced with a knowledge of 'spiceosome dynamics' whether I like it or not. *Mutability* is a reality at the fingertips of 'human hands', overstepping even Darwin. Is this virus a mutant and does the cure rely on a genetic mutant vector? Can that be true? Social media was innocently a technological advance for speedy delivery to network with friends and family. Yet, are the mutant algorithms (non-transparent) in social media giant tools to possibly send us down rabbit holes to 'false friends' for profitability anonymously? In some cases, even creating possible rifts between families and friends? Can this be true? Are all of the above true? Are none of the above true? Are all false? No answer is universal. Is disinformation in digital media a *new* normal or a mutant?

The spectacle of the circus has existed for centuries, with peddlers of 'snake oil' cures (disinformation) allowed to speak freely in public forums around the tents. The circus was a distraction to relieve boredom, and often based on human curiosity, even to a mocking default. Who questioned those decisions back then? Have we come so far as to *not even* recognize ourselves in line at the circus? Am I standing outside in line at the modern circus, curious in pursuit of knowledge? Am I any different from Mary's Victor Frankenstein? The old proverb stands out: "Curiosity killed the cat". Can I make ethical choices before I slip into the "rabbit hole"?

How can I draw the line on my own 'curiosity' for knowledge, in the information/dis-information age? These are my own ethical questions I face today. As ancient yogis practiced the limits of the body to control the mind, perhaps now I am called to practice the limits of the mind to control my own body---human hand (*clicking the mouse*). Turning on the electricity switch with his own hand was Dr Frankenstein's choice, and later he tried to rectify his own faulty decision. Was he successful? At least he tried! He collected his pieces of an unfinished experiment, a replica of the first investigation. Only then after the disaster of the first experiment, he no longer wanted to verify his hypothesis as a scientist with replication data to confirm. He had already calculated the risk of the answer; *unknown consequences.* He threw it into the sea, sending it back to the giver of life! He was no longer in wanton to be a doctor, a chemist, a 'creator'. He longed to live his life in peace, as a commoner. He was ready to re-join the human race. In some fashion, he buried Dr Frankenstein, himself.

I suppose this will be my new path in following Mary's warning; stepping into her footsteps to ethics for a *new* age, especially after 2019/ 2020. I return to Pierce Shelley's poem.

> *It is the same: for, be it joy or sorrow,*
> *The path of its departure still is free.*
> *Man's yesterday may ne'er be like his morrow;*
> *'Nought may endure but mutability!'*

25

Krack*

Mary Shelley Wollstonecraft lived the summer of doom 1816 confined largely by Nature---thunder and lightning--- constantly ravishing the hopes of a "normal" holiday that imposed Europeans to stay at home or indoors. Lord Byron suggests writing ghost stories to the group of writers he hosted to enjoy a getaway from Victorian England in Switzerland that summer, Mary Wollstonecraft included. The setting to this unique proposal was framed by an unusual freak of Nature, a gargantuan volcanic eruption on the other side of the world in Indonesia had erupted in 1815 sending a cloud of gloom (ashes) circulating the air stream for a year. It was claimed that Mother Nature burst open her seams from the deepest trenches of the sea, reverberating so loud that it was heard around the world, CRACK!

The Krack*

T'was the "krack" before dawn
heard 'round the world,
Earthquake *daemon* danced and swirled,
Beneath a rift at sea
Far far away in Indonesia, no less
Sunless, darkness, unlocked the key
Beauty of the Beast had summoned Mary,
Krack! Its face of crevices arises, ---scary,
Unfathomable deeps of fire and ice
She wrote and wrought the tail of a creature
All night, and yet day never arrived---
even the SUN was brooding, depressed,
this no man, no woman's land---a desert of gloom
looming in air, reverberating ONE
Krack!
A wave pierced HER eardrums, rattled in the twilight
Mary dreamt in uneasy slumber
Woken beyond a doubt
Earth was changing, Nature began its revolt
At the hands of a Doctor, or was it a lab technician?
Krack!
Dull yellow eye, she concocts, with a simple electric wave
 to rouse its limbs.
Catastrophe, wretch---a monster was born, a star
North Star shifted in the sky to make room,
What had she, Mary, Wollstone-crafted to form?
1819, herstory, revealed to the world,
Dr Frankenstein hands at play in a lab,
2019, our story, begins, where she left off,
Krack! Covid-19 heard 'round the world.

KRACK ("Key Reinstallation Attack") is a replay attack (a type of exploitable flaw) on the Wi-Fi Protected Access protocol that secures Wi-Fi connections. It was discovered in 2016 by the Belgian researchers Mathy Vanhoef and Frank Piessens of the University of Leuve.

Melting Mont Blanc
R. Ruiz Scarfuto 2019

26

Muted Mutability

Mary Shelley uses the term "mutability" only once in her travel diary in describing her encounter of a literary landmark of Rousseau:

"Here a small obelisk is erected to the glory of Rousseau, and here (such is the mutability of human life) the magistrates, the successors of those who exiled him from his native country, were shot by the populace during that revolution, which his writings mainly contributed to mature, and which, notwithstanding the temporary bloodshed and injustice with which it was polluted, has produced enduring benefits to mankind, which all the chicanery of statesmen, nor even the great conspiracy of kings, can entirely render vain. From respect to the memory of their predecessors, none of the present magistrates ever walk in Plainpalais." (History of Six Weeks' Tour, p. 101)

Note: The following is based on poems presented in *Frankenstein* and scientific abstracts about mutability, then intermingled with my own lines as a replay on the original texts (See end of poem for references).

Muted mutability

Muted mutability
Shall never hang her cloak
On the shoulders,
Of the dwarfed
illuminati,
human shield.

Ghastly, and scarr'd, and riven.—Is this the scene
Where the old Earthquake-daemon taught her young
Ruin? Were these their toys? or did a sea
Of fire envelop once this silent snow?

"As a mutation,
more likely
to disrupt--- an interaction
than to form---
a new one,"

We rest;
a dream has power--- to poison sleep.
We rise;
We feel, conceive, or reason;
laugh or weep,

Like one who, on a lonely road,
Doth walk in fear and dread,

Ghastly, obvious,
doomed to ruin?
virus strikes the hour,
reverberating

from the bell towers
once, twice, thrice---
ad infinitum?
from Notre Dame of Paris
to St. Peter's of New York
ringing in my ear---
an echo heard 'round the world,
on one forgotten day,
December 2020.

From yon remotest waste, have overthrown
The limits of the dead and living world,
Never to be reclaimed. The dwelling-place
Of insects, beasts, and birds, becomes its spoil;

"It is likely
that relative stabilization
takes the form of destabilization,

Embrace fond woe, or cast our cares away;
one wand'ring thought pollutes the day.

Their food and their retreat for ever gone,
So much of life and joy is lost. The race
Of man, flies far in dread his work and dwelling
Vanish, like smoke before the tempest's stream.

of the competing
conformation,

And, having once turned round, walks on,
And turns no more his head;
It is the same: for, be it joy or sorrow,
The path of its departure still is free.

And their place is not known. Below, vast caves
Shine in the rushing torrent's restless gleam,
Which from those secret chasms in tumult welling
Meet in the vale, and one majestic River,

Because he knows a frightful fiend
Doth close behind him tread.

Early February 2021,
church bells 'nought endure',
ceased to ring upon the hour,
cease to ring at all.

The breath and blood of distant lands, for ever
Rolls its loud waters to the ocean waves,
Breathes its swift vapours to the circling air.[1]

None can reply—all seems eternal now.
The wilderness has a mysterious tongue
Which teaches awful doubt, or faith so mild,

No more willing,
To attend---not even daring dwarfs
Human shields lay at the door,
No longer restless,
Only still.
Beneath the sacred arches,
Silently, the ghosts exhale,
'swift vapours to the circling air'

"At present, however,
molecular basis of the action,

So solemn, so serene, that man may be,
But for such faith, with Nature reconcil'd;

of these general suppressor
mutations--- is unknown."

Man's yesterday may ne'er be like his morrow;
Nought may endure but mutability!

Infiniti---Illuminati
Do we dare ask?

When shall Thee, Creator mine,
'Shine in the rushing torrent'
To mute the mutability?

Original Texts:

"As a mutation
 is more likely to disrupt an interaction
than to form a new one,
 it is likely
 that relative stabilization
 takes the form of destabilization
of the competing
 conformation,
At present, however,
the molecular basis of the action
of these general suppressor mutations
 is unknown."
"'Nought May Endure but Mutability': Spliceosome Dynamics and the
Regulation of Splicing"
[Duncan]

We are as clouds that veil the midnight moon;
  How restlessly they speed, and gleam, and quiver,
Streaking the darkness radiantly!—yet soon
  Night closes round, and they are lost for ever:

Or like forgotten lyres, whose dissonant strings
  Give various response to each varying blast,
To whose frail frame no second motion brings
  One mood or modulation like the last.

We rest.—A dream has power to poison sleep;
  We rise.—One wandering thought pollutes the day;
We feel, conceive or reason, laugh or weep;
  Embrace fond woe, or cast our cares away:
It is the same!—For, be it joy or sorrow,

The path of its departure still is free:
Man's yesterday may ne'er be like his morrow;
Nought may endure but Mutability.

"Mutability"[**Percy Bysshe Shelley**]

Like one who, on a lonely road,
Doth walk in fear and dread,
And, having once turned round, walks on,
And turns no more his head;
Because he knows a frightful fiend
Doth close behind him tread.

"The Rime of the Ancient Mariner"
[**Samuel Taylor Coleridge**]

From yon remotest waste, have overthrown
The limits of the dead and living world,
Never to be reclaimed. The dwelling-place
Of insects, beasts, and birds, becomes its spoil;
Their food and their retreat for ever gone,
So much of life and joy is lost. The race
Of man, flies far in dread his work and dwelling
Vanish, like smoke before the tempest's stream.
And their place is not known. Below, vast caves
Shine in the rushing torrent's restless gleam,
Which from those secret chasms in tumult welling
Meet in the vale, and one majestic River,
The breath and blood of distant lands, for ever
Rolls its loud waters to the ocean waves,
Breathes its swift vapours to the circling air.

"Mont Blanc" [**Percy Bysshe Shelley**]

Muted mutability?

Muted mutability
Shall never hang her cloak
On the shoulders,
Of the dwarfed
illuminati,
human shield
to Infinitus.

Ghastly, obvious,
 doomed to ruin?
virus strikes the hour,
reverberating
 from the bell towers
once, twice, thrice---
ad infinitum?
from Notre Dame of Paris
 to St. Peter's of New York
ringing in my ear---
an echo heard 'round the world,
on one forgotten day,
December 2020.

I.

Early in February 2021,
church bells 'nought endure',
ceased to ring upon the hour,
cease to ring at all.

No more willing,
To attend---not even daring dwarfs
Human shields lay at the door,

No longer restless,
Only still.

Beneath the sacred arches,
Silently, the ghosts exhale,
'swift vapours to the circling air'

Infiniti---Illuminati
Do we dare ask?

When shall our Creator,
'Shine in the rushing torrent'
To mute the mutability?

"Muted Mutability" **[Rosalinda Ruiz Scarfuto]**

27

Lista de Poemas

1.-Oda a Mary Shelley

2-Reina de Aiguilles Mont Blanc

3-Los amantes de las cumbres

4-Pilar de pinos

5-Sendero bajo sus hongos

6- Cueva de hielo

7- Mutabilidad

8-El Krack

28

Los amantes de las cumbres

I.
Debajo
del domo
De arcos de catedral
bóveda encima
Un corazón
entre ellos
Shelley y Shelley
Navegando mares, incluso ríos
Timones inquietos en lagos ondulados
Pasando por arroyos revueltos, y gargantas rocosas
Torrente de cascadas, rociadas con frescura
Despertando a sus almas, ungiéndolas
En un viaje, que llamaron
La seis semanas de gira

II.

vehemente trama
y alrededor su templo
los Alpes
divino destino
músicas de la pradera
charlas de insectos, colmenas
mezclaron se bien a la sombra de árboles
como tiernas plantitas
restaurando antiguos bosques
vaivén de flores silvestres, apenas vistas
misterio cromático, tierra firme
cercana a Julie y Saint-Preux
que fortaleció su amor
Como marido y mujer
Una amistad forjada
entre poetas primaverales
y letras que escribieron
Uno y verso

III.

Bajo un mismo cielo contemplan
sus plumas, mientras sueñan
más de uno a otro
y-aún-así (aun así)
Juntos, al unísono, separados
La naturaleza los atrajo hacia Ella
un hechizo lanzado mucho antes
En el umbral
Del vicio humano
Seducido
"¡explora!"
más allá de su tierra
ancestral

IV.

Sus corazones
un mero testimonio
Mientras juntos se sumergen
se abre camino Neptuno
desde lo bajo
liberándose de la oscuridad
Aurora anhela mostrarse
desde lo alto, liberada
del cautiverio

V.

Las nubes se abren
Las confesiones rugen
Como es arriba, es abajo
oídos desnudos
revelan
al ojo desnudo
Ruptura
normas sociales
dioses y diosas
el descubridor, descubierto
él mismo
ella misma
uno

VI.

Compelido
por ninguna otra otredad
entre femenino y masculino
Intuición interior
fuego volcánico, espiral
girando grieta del océano

su encanto
liberado
Tierra límpida
de nuevo
renacida

VII.
Mientras Pierce Shelley
alude a lo sombrío de la Naturaleza
Mary nos exalta hacia adelante
para reconocer nuestra sombra
la mente humana
en la pared, ella misma
sin duda Platón
Líricamente poético
Cantó con el arpa de Sapho
sublime fuerza de la naturaleza
entre ellos
Los amantes
Apretados como flores silvestres
impresos en un libro
de pálidos colores, mermado
ser o no ser
a toda costa

VIII.
Una prueba crucial para nuestra mente
Cerebro izquierdo y derecho
electrocutado
en un asedio paralizante
Un asedio que estalla
por las comisuras del amor
otro lado nuestro
uno mismo.

IX.

El amor
de la Naturaleza
el Amor
de la locura
amor que tan mal se ha ido
y sin embargo, pervive
entre sus páginas
como fragante fragmento
tan fresco como las flores silvestres arrancadas
de años que se fueron, intactas

X.

De
su
imaginación,
reverberando inmóvil
Bajo esta Cúpula
De vitrales
rotos
Arcos de catedral
Ya no
protegen
protegen
la belleza,
comprometida
no he olvidado
La liturgia del amor
Apenas
des-cubierta
La nieve y el hielo
En su imagen

Todavía
fresca
una vez,
sentados
juntos
Un trono
Canto de los Cantos

XI.

Puesto que
los renglones de los amantes
atraviesan hoy mi corazón
admito, siento
nuevas y boyantes auras
flotando en las olas
con la armonía de las arpas
descuerdadas, descantadas
para llenar las sombras
de los Amantes.

29

Pilar de Pinos: un susurro desde el hueco del árbol

Breath of Pine, I feel refreshed
Aliento a pino, me siento renovado
Your roots here, now
Aquí y ahora tus raíces
so bolden to survive,
se atreven a sobrevivir
reaching deep inside
llegando tan profundo en la tierra
the Earth, that I am ALIVE!
que estoy VIVO
through the thicket, bramble, ramble
a través de la espesura, de la zarza, del desvarío
of my mind, collecting every sense
de mi mente, amasando tantos sentidos
even nonsense fills my body
que hasta el sinsentido llena mi cuerpo
on this trail,
en este camino,

As I gasp for every breath!
¡mientras jadeo por cada aliento!

I ask you now:
Ahora te pregunto:
"Is it true that Mary passed you by?
"¿Es cierto que María pasó de largo?
200 years ago! Perhaps a seedling,
¡Hace 200 años! Tal vez una semilla,
she once saw You?
¿alguna vez te vio?
No doubt You have matured,
sin duda has madurado
beyond my years and hers,
más allá de mis años y de los suyos,
I am humiliated,
Me siento humillada
For today, You, hold up,
Porque hoy, Tú, te sostienes,
this Mountain, no small feat! Mont Blanc!
esta montaña, es cosa seria. ¡Mont Blanc!
From within my body, mind and Soul!
¡Desde dentro de mi cuerpo, mente y alma!
I am humbled at Your feet.
Me rindo a tus pies
Knotted, gnarled, bark
resinosa, anudada, enredada,
Trunk of painful marks
Tronco de marcas dolorosas
twisted years of journey
años de perversa travesía
through, and through
buscando límites

I see, I feel, I listen
Veo, siento, escucho
To your Soul, Be True.
A tu alma, sé fiel.

Towering
imponente

over me, a tiny poet,
sobre mí, una pequeña poetisa
I am here, far below,
Estoy aquí, muy abajo,
scattered mind
mi mente dispersa
like autumn leaves
como hojas de otoño
randomly
al azar
I stop.
Me detengo

Please
Por favor
speak to me
háblame
for only you can tell your story,
porque solo tu puedes contar tu historia,
true,
cierto
For when you fall
porque cuando caigas
I may not be here, no one at all.
Puede que yo no esté aquí, ni nadie en absoluto.

Who will listen then?
¿Quién escuchará entonces?

I lay down
Me acuesto
On the Earth
En la tierra
Waiting for response...
Esperando una respuesta...
a rushing pulse within the roots
un pulso acelerado dentro de las raíces
begins to pound!
¡comienza a latir!

Hear me now *Poet:*
Escúchame ahora Poetisa:

"Sediments
"Los sedimentos
Began to crumble
Comenzaron a caer
with every glacier
con cada glaciar
melting faster than before
derritiéndose más rápido que antes
across the *seven* seas,
a través de los siete mares
cutting ice like the sacred butcher
cortando el hielo como el carnicero sagrado
warning me, my sisters, brothers
advirtiéndome, mis hermanas, hermanos

to beware
que tenga cuidado
all the forests, falling down!"
de todos los bosques, que se están cayendo!"

We heard the wind,
Oímos al viento,
Ripping through, our hollows
Desgarrar nuestras huecos
blowing in our ears,
soplando en nuestros oídos,
rattling all our branches,
sonajeando todas nuestras ramas,
we feared the end
y temimos que el fin
was near."
estaba cerca

A voice began to speak:
Una voz comenzó a hablar:

'It is hidden in the core,
"está escondido en el mero centro
you must go far beneath,
habrás de ir hasta lo profundo
to find your precious rock
para encontrar tu piedra preciosa
your bedrock in the storm.'
tu lecho de roca en la tormenta

"I dug into the core,
Excavé hacia el corazón
Centre of our Earth
el centro de nuestra Tierra

Day by Day
día a día
Night by Night
noche a noche
I did not stop
no paré
My roots exhausted
mis raíces exhaustas
But I would not let them rest.
Pero no podía dejarlas descansar
Until I found
hasta que hallara
My rock, behold!"
mi piedra, hela aquí!"

"*Mother*, I wept
"Madre, he llorado
Help me!
Ayúdame!
I am tired, broken,
estoy cansada, rota
and so frail,
y tan frágil,
I feel so very lonely,
me siento tan sola,
I haven't even seedlings,
Ni siquiera tengo plantitas
to replace me, when I fall."
para reemplazarme, cuando caiga".

"*She* nourished me,
"Ella me alimentó,
made me stronger
me hizo más fuerte

with *Her* precious minerals,
con sus preciosos minerales,
Kept me solid, bold, and strong,
Me mantuvo sólida, audaz y fuerte,
After many months below
Después de muchos meses abajo
She announced:
Ella anunció:
'Time
Es el momento
for you
para ti
to stand tall
de mantenerte firme
Above
Por encima
as an Elder
como abuela
of your tribe,
de la tribu
you must call a poet---
debes llamar a un poeta...
To come and dance, again
Para que venga y baile, de nuevo
Around your trunk,
alrededor de tu tronco
Only then,
Sólo entonces,
the seedlings will
las plantitas regresarán
return, and you
y tú
can once again
una vez más puedes

rejoice in birth reborn.
regocijarse en el nacimiento renacido.
Upon the poets'
Sobre los poetas
lips I will send
enviaré labios
my muse
para cantar
to sing.'
musa mía

I,
Yo
your poet,
tu poeta

called,
llamado,
today.
hoy
My footsteps
mis huellas
summoned
convocadas
from the bedrock
desde el lecho de roca
core?
Corazón?

"The column you see today,
"La columna que hoy ves
Comes from far beneath
viene de abajo

Truth be told,
a decir verdad
So Above,
Como arriba
So Below,
Como abajo

So Be it!
Que así sea!
I
Yo
AM"
Soy
Me, the poet,
Yo, la poeta
Suddenly, heard an echo through the roots,
De repente, escuché un eco a través de las raíces,
A shock wave pierced my ear
Una onda expansiva atravesó mi oído
I had to lift my tiny head
Tuve que levantar mi cabecita
To save my brain from bursting forth,
Para salvar a mi cerebro de estallar
Then suddenly from
Entonces, de repente,
High above
desde lo alto
Came
llegó
A
una
Voice
voz

"I have waited"
"He esperado"
For you my *friend*,
por ti, amiga mía,
a poet of the forest,
poeta del bosque
I did call you
Te he llamado
As my MOTHER said."
Como dijo mi MADRE

I, the poet was confused.
Yo, la poeta estaba confundida.

"For I your pillar PINE has not fallen
"Para mí tu pilar de pinos no ha caído
but look I have no seedlings!
pero mira que no tengo plantitas
My shade is wasted on a barren
Mi sombra se desperdicia en un estéril
trail of runners.
rastro de corredores.
I fear I will but disappear
Temo que desapareceré
Forever, leaving you, the poets
Por siempre, dejándolos a ustedes, los poetas
With nothing, to inspire.
Sin nada, para inspirar.
I had hoped someday
Tenía la esperanza de que algún día
My call
would be heard
**Mi llamado
sería atendido**

Even though, it is quite muted
Aunque, sea bastante silencioso
By the rushing waters, melting fast
Por las aguas turbulentas, derritiéndose con prisa
my bedrock, homeland, siphoned last
mi lecho de roca, mi patria, succionadas
reduced, but I refused to quit.
reducido, pero me negué a renunciar
I summoned on the Moon
Convoqué a la luna
To spread my call
Para difundir mi llamada
So, you came
Entonces, viniste
Daughter
hija
of
de
Moonlight
luz de luna
glow.
resplandor.

I, the poet
Yo, el poeta
saw the branches sway
vi el balanceo de las ramas
for now, the wind
porque ahora, el viento
joined in
unido
the mighty rattle
en la sonaja poderosa

frightened me
me asustó
I turned and hugged
Me di la vuelta y me abracé
My pillar Pine.
Mi pino pinar

"Yes!
Sí!
Ms. Mary Shelley
Señora Mary Shelley
wrote of Me! A seedling, once.
escribió de mí! Una plantita. una vez,.
She was here, with my friends,
Ella estuvo aquí, con mis amigos,
She mingled, mused and laughed
Ella se mezcló, musitó y rió
In my father's shade"
A la sombra de mi padre

I, smiled---with no response,
Yo, sonreí... sin respuesta,
For fear my ears
Por miedo a que mis oídos
May be forever
pudieran para siempre
deaf.
ensordecer

"I am alone,
Estoy sola
I am no longer
Ya no estoy

At the centre of your dance
Al centro de tu danza
Where once your mothers, fathers,
Donde una vez tus madres, padres,
brothers, sisters
hermanos, hermanas
gathered in sacred clothes
se reunieron con sagrados atavíos
singing 'round my trunk
cantando alrededor de mi tronco
with seeds on ankles
con semillas en los tobillos
to celebrate
para celebrar
the season change
El cambio de estación.

I felt the pain,
Sentí el dolor
this mighty being---so eloquently revealed
este poderoso ser--tan elocuentemente revelado
I held on---hoping my embrace
Me aferré--esperando que mi abrazo
could soothe, a broken heart, so immense.
pudiera calmar, un corazón roto, tan inmenso.

"OH! I miss
"¡Oh! extraño
Their Songs of Joy
Sus canciones de alegría
Turning with the leaves
Girando con las hojas
Once shared, together, you and I
Una vez compartimos, tú y yo, juntos

On strings of harps,
En las cuerdas de las arpas
On human voice
En la voz humana
Rejoicing of the Mother."
Regocijo de la Madre

I, the poet,
Yo, la poeta
Slowly, reached up, and whispered
lentamente, me acerqué y susurré
In its friendly hollowl;
En su amistoso hueco

"Oh,
Oh
Mighty Pine!
Poderoso pino
I *am* so sorry
lo siento tanto
We have forgotten
Nos hemos olvidado
To sing the songs
cantar las canciones
upon this mountain face
sobre esta cara de la montaña
to honour cornerstones
para honrar las piedras angulares
unseen, beneath your trunk
que no se ven, bajo tu tronco
That every breath, you take,
que cada vez que respiras
to push your roots, below

para empujar hacia abajo tus raíces,
Giveth us the strength to create, to live!
nos da la fuerza para crear, para vivir
On solid ground
En tierra firme
As I gasp for my tiny breath---
Mientras jadeo por mi débil aliento...
On this very trail,
En este mismo camino,

I admit
admito
I had not noticed
No me había percatado
An absence of those seedlings,
de la ausencia de las plantitas
children of the forest---shame on me!
hijos del bosque... ¡qué vergüenza!
Your last breath, a call,
Su último aliento, una llamada,
your very last!
¡tu último!
Expired
Caducado
Has not gone
No se ha ido
In vain."
en vano
I, the poet began to dance
empezé a danzar Yo, la poetisa
Around the trunk
alrededor del tronco
With sacred song
Con un canto sagrado

Magically my lips
Mágicamente mis labios
could sing!
podían cantar!
To celebrate
para celebrar
this Pillar Pine
a este pino pilar
Divine.
divino
I think, I saw
Creo que vi
Mother Spider
a la madre araña
Crawl out from darkness
Arrastrarse desde la oscuridad
Hidden deep within old Pine's hollow knoll
Escondida en lo profundo de la antiguo hueco del Pino
its tiny---legs began to wave,
sus diminutas patas comenzaron a agitarse
A-mused, A-mazed
A-legrada, A-sombrada
I hope the Pain
Espero que el dolor
Is soothed
Se calma
Away
Y se vaya
Be Forgotten
Y sea olvidado
Knot! (Not),
Nudo (No),
nought
nada

Whisper in the Pine Knoll
R. Ruiz Scarfuto 2019

30

Sendero hacia los hongos, bajo sus lamelas

I.

Frolicking along the mountain path---stone by stone
> **Retozando camino a la montaña… piedra a piedra**

Mont Blanc, a stone's throw away.
> **Mont Blanc, un tiro de piedra**

Up along---over a bramble, a steady runner's joy---
> **A lo largo---encima de una zarza, la alegría de un corredor constante**

Passing me with pen in hand taking stock
> **haciendo balance pluma en mano**

Of details too small to notice
> **de detalles tan nimios que ni se ven**

If you scurry, like a rabbit.
si como un conejo te escabuyes

Let them run ragged,
andarás cansado mientras huyes

I am content to wallow
Me conformo con revolcarme

In the shadow of a mushroom gill,
A la sombra de las branquias de un hongo

For beneath the beaten path---blink you'd miss it!
Pues bajo el gastado sendero --- ¡algo parpadea!

Nature's harmony---beauty---
Armonía de la naturaleza, belleza
A pageant of colours only Lewis Carroll would know
Un desfile de colores sólo para Lewis Carroll
Absolutely psychedelic---I pinch myself---
Absoluta psicodelia... me pellizco...
To be sure I'm still in this reality.
Para ver si aún estoy en esta realidad.

Never never have I been so full of wonder---wonder full!
**Nunca estuve tan llena de asombro
-¡asombroso!**

Teeter totter on my---tiny---scale
haciendo columpio en mi escal, ita

profusely abundant, these wonder cakes,
estos pasteles, abundantes en maravillas

desserts in Nature, displayed for all?
  postres por la Naturaleza, ¿para todos?

Spreading joy to only those on slower pace:
  Infundiendo alegría al de paso quedo

  STOP, TURN 'ROUND...
  PARA, DA, LA VUELTA...

Moving back, to glimpse, a slow dance
  hacia atrás, para vislumbrar, una danza lenta

Watch, how they stand---firm
Mira, cómo se mantienen firmes

Apparently, still.
Todavía, al parecer

  Surely, they are growing
  Seguro, están creciendo

Changing---transforming
Cambiando--transformando
  FORM,
  forma
FORMED,
formado
 MORPHED
mutado
 META,
meta
METAMORPHIC
metamórfico

DE-COMPOSURE (*without* composure)
Des-compostura (sin compostura)
FORM-LESS
sin forma
UNFORMED
sin formar
NO-THING (nothing)
sin nada (nada)

Forrest floor richer
suelo del bosque más rico
Tumble, a fallen tree
un árbol caído, cae
lay down, gracefully
recostado, con gracia
Who heard it?
¿Quién lo ha oído?
Pierce the Heart,
Perfora el corazón
not even I wept, for its fall.
Ni siquiera lloré por su caída.
Now destined for compost
destinado ahora al abono
      Fungi meticulously
los hongos meticulosos
Appear, Tasks to finish
Aparecen, tareas por hacer
 I, a witness
Yo, testigo

Of a palette richer
De una exhuberante paleta
orange so vibrant, red so robust
naranja tan vibrante, y rojo tan fuerte
Blinds me so.
Me ciegan

II.
I lay down
Me acuesto

on the forest floor,
sobre la cama del bosque
rugged rocks pinch my spine
pedruscos pican mi espina
like the giant Pine, grave.
Como el pino gigante, sepulcral

A pine once seen
Un pino que una vez
By Mary 200 yesterday's ago?
¿vio Mary hace 200 años?

Here, under the mushroom gills
Aquí, bajo las lamelas
Fascinated, I am
Fascinada, estoy
By the world, underside,
Por el mundo, debajo
upside down, downside up
al revés, al derecho
With my fungi friends.
Con mis amigos hongos

careful,
diligentes
tricky
jaraneros
not to touch!
¡No tocar!
Even *Alice*, took notice of a bottle
Incluso Alice, apreció una botella.

Before she lifted the liquid, "Drink me"
Antes que levantara el líquido, "Bébeme"
Was it labelled, poison?
¿se suponía que era veneno?
I am no expert on fatal edibles,
No soy experto en comestibles que matan
Spores of Poison,
Esporas de veneno
Spread freely on airwaves,
Esparcidas libres como ondas
I am not testing
No voy a probar,
or wanton to know
o a querer saber

by my own experiment.
por mi propio experimento.
Ancestors, intuitive,
Intuitivos, ancestros
Listened to Nature's call
Escuché la llamada de la naturaleza
Beware! I hear them echo!
¡Cuidado! ¡Oigo su eco!

Frozen, bending my head, lower
Congelada, agachando mi cabeza
My lips silent, until my own eyes,
Mis labios en silencio, hasta que mis propios ojos
Are open, She reveals, her treasure...
Se abran, y Ella revele, su tesoro...
Under the Gills---a world unto itself
Bajo las lamelas--- un mundo en sí mismo
I gasp!
¡Jadeo!
Delicate
Dalicada
Rigid
rígida
Harmonious
armoniosa
Random
fortuita
flexible
flexible

Is there a beauty
Sí hay una belleza
So perfectly
tan perfecta
Aligned.
alineada

So attractive
Tan atractiva
to 'touch'
de tocar
NO! I mustn't!
¡No, no debo!

I shy away...
me retraigo
Respecting HER
Respetándola
underside
inclinada
Her nameless, jewel
Su joya sin nombre

A fine art
Un bello arte
gallery
galería
to admire
para admirar

up close,
de cerca

but far
pero lejos
from touch!
¡De tocar!
I dare not to disturb
No me atrevo a irrumpir
Whence She sprays me
Desde donde me rocía
With her spores---
Con sus esporas...

A mere step out
Un simple paso al frente

Of the beaten runner's path
De la gastada senda del corredor
Nature so nonchalant, waiting for us
naturaleza en calma, espera por nosotros
To slow down,
para ir despacio
Ancient, as tainted bronze
Antigua, como bronce manchado
On unused urns,
En urnas sin usar
a reservoir of *herstory*---
un depósito de *su historia*

evolutionary
evolutiva
metaphysics meets biology,
metafísica con biología,

I am captive,
Estoy cautiva

in Her class---a charm bracelet
en SU clase, un brazalete
made of gems
hecho de joyas,
dotted, hidden, in someone's
country side.
salpicado, oculto
en la tierra de alguien.

I wake up from my day dream,
despierto de mi sueño
Where have I been?
¿Dónde estuve?

Visiting a foreign land, as Gulliver,
como Gulliver, visitando tierras lejanas
I met the Yahoos, and You!
¡Conocí a los Yahoos y a ustedes!

My mushroom *friends*!
Mis amigos hongos
Stepping away, ever so slowly,
Alejándose, tan lentamente,
As I came---promising,
Como vine, prometiendo,
"Tomorrow I'll be back."
"mañana volveré"

III.

T' was tomorrow
Ya era mañana
Had I not been
Si no hubiera estado
Just here---there?
Justo aquí, ¿ahí?
Under this tree,
bajo este árbol
Around this bend.
Alrededor de esta curva
Was it *impossible* to return?
¿Fue imposible regresar?
Overnight---the gills have dis-appeared?
¿des-aparecieron las lamelas por la noche?
She fooled me---Had I been imagining?
Ella me engañó, ¿lo había imaginado?
Was it a one-way ticket?
¿Era un billete solo de ida?

Oh please, appear!
¡por favor aparece!
She had stamped me
Ella me había estampado
 in the memory gills
en la memoria de las lamelas
 of my mind/nebulous
nebulosas de mi mente
entity---not even I know where YOU live?
Entidad, ¿ni siquiera yo sé dónde vives?

Whoosh---a sudden breeze,
brisa repentina, un susurro
Quickly I step away
me alejo de prisa
     A Flash
     un destello
     A Neon passer-by
     Un transeúnte de neón
     A Runner, no doubt.
     Sin duda, un corredor
Once more---missing out
otra vez no aprovechado
Nature's Art!
¡Arte de la naturaleza!

As I *turned* back
Cuando me di la vuelta

My eye captured
Mi ojo captó
A glimpse---there She is!
Un atisbo... ¡y hela aquí!

So proud, So tall---
Tan orgullosa, tan alta...
amongst Her miniatures.
entre sus miniaturas

I slowly move to greet Her
Me muevo lenta y la saludo
Quietly, I lay down
me recuesto en silencio
with golden charcoal
con carbón dorado
slivers prickly on my forearm
picudas astillas en mi antebrazo

I look up, to Her door,
Miro arriba, Su umbral
I am at Her doorstep,
Estoy a sus puertas

She opens her Heart, "Morning!"
Ella abre su corazón, "¡Buenos días!"
I think I saw her gills twitch?
Creo que vi sus lamelas temblar
"Hello again—It's me"
"Hola de nuevo, soy yo"

Sun is glinting
el sol centella
Reflecting—my eyelids blink
reflejando, mis párpados guiñan
Once again
de nuevo

I enter in
entro en
Wonderland
un mundo maravilloso
Lewis
Lewis
called her Alice
la llamó Alicia
I call her nothing
Yo no la llamo nada
We need not speak
No necesitamos hablar
I am under
yo estoy debajo
 the gills
 de las lamelas
         with Her
         junto a su
 mushroom
 tribu
    tribe.
    de hongos

IV.

Time
El tiempo
stops.
Se para
I am, no longer human,
ya no soy, humana
I am humane.
Soy humanitaria

Runners, run,
los corredores, corren
while Poets---pause
mientras los poetas, pausan
Sensing heartbeats---
perciven latidos
animate, inanimate
animados, inanimados
Rocks rumble,
retumban las rocas
mountains decompose
las montañas decaen
under the gaze of spore-a-tic, (spores)
bajo la mirada de lo espora-di-co (esporas)

She is all dressed up, today.
Ella hoy viste de gala
Her gills all pressed, pristine
Todas sus lamelas prensadas, prístinas
Ready for a tea party, I suppose.
Supongo, que listas para tomar el té
I am in a day dreamy mood---
Estoy en un estado de ánimo de ensueño
Calm with hues unspoken,
calma de tonos silenciosos
She winks---?
¿Ella parpadea?
Ah! Must I really *get up*
¡Eh! ¿De veras debo levantarme?
from down under here?
¿de aquí debajo?

Hongo y sus lamelas
R. Ruiz Scarfuto 2019

3 1

La Cueva de hielo

I am
> *Yo soy*

forbidden follower
> *seguidora prohibida*

of foreshadowed Mary
> *de María la del vislumbro*

Forgiven not----
> *no perdonada*

Forebode
> *Augurio*

Once, a Glacier Sea.
> *Una vez, mar glaciar.*

Now, a thawing river dance,
> *Ahora, un deshielo danza el río*

Faster than even SHE, can dance
> *Más rápido de lo que ella puede danzar*

Exposed---unveiled
> *Expuesta --- desvelada*

As a bride on wedding night
> *Como una novia en la noche de bodas*

Frightened, frozen,
> *Asustada, congelada*
down, down, down
> *abajo abajo abajo*
the mountain,
> *la montaña*
her dress has fallen
> *su vestido ha caído*
slip sliding away.
> *Desliz que se desliza*

SHE, alone,
> *ELLA, sola*
retreats, here
> *aquí, se retira*
inside the ICE CAVE!
> *¡dentro de la CUEVA DE HIELO!*

Deafening glimpse awaits me!
> *Me espera un atisbo ensordecedor*
Ignited---Whirling neurons
> *Encendido… Neuronas arremolinadas*
Massive synapses
> *Sinapsis masivas*
doors unhinged,
> *puertas desgajadas,*
locks be broken,
> *cerraduras rotas*

My SELF, of frozen
> *Mi yo,*
> *de congelados pensamientos*
thoughts---dare I step inside?
> *¿me atreveré a entrar?*

to break HER silent retreat?
>*¿Y romper su retiro silencioso?*

Sapphire,
>*Zafiro*
crystal BLUE
>*azul cristalino*
a terrific aura emits
>*exhala un aura fantástica*
from a side of Mont Blanc
>*desde un lado del Mont Blanc,*

We have come
>*Hemos venido*
To awaken HER
>*A despertarla*
Ghastly proposal
>*temible propuesta*
I dare to say.
>*Me atrevo a decir.*

Above me,
>*Por encima de mí*
Ice-cycles
>*Ciclos de hielo*
hang like tears
>*cuelgan como lágrimas*
Below me,
>*Debajo de mí*
Ice age
>*La edad de hielo*
melting years.
>*años se derriten*

YOUR ice-warming Womb,
       Su vientre que calienta el hielo,
Sanctum revealed,
       Sanctum revelado,
Into your cavern,
       En tu caverna
¿Shall I roam?
       ¿He de vagar?

I tip toe,
       de puntillas
over fringe of gate,
       sobre el borde de la puerta,
I gasp!
       ¡jadeo!

I am follower
       soy una seguidora
Not too sure,
       no muy segura
Down, Down, Down,
       Abajo, Abajo, Abajo,
the corridor AZURE.
       el corredor AZURE

whizzing by
       zumbando

photos clicking,
       clics de fotos
selfies---frozen
       selfies congelados

bye, bye,
>   *adiós*
birdie,
>   *pajarito,*
bye, bye
>   *adiós*
I sigh!
>   *¡Suspiro!*
Dare to touch
>   *Atreverse a tocar*
YOUR chilling walls
>   *Sus escalofriantes paredes*
Tap, tap, tap
>   *Tap, tap, tap*
YOU capture me,
>   *me captura,*
My fingertips,
>   *las yemas de mis dedos*
sticking
>   *pegoteándose*
on YOUR icy walls,
>   *en SUS gélidos muros*
My fingerprint,
>   *Mi huella dactilar*
forever, plastered
>   *por siempre plasmada*
in time bygone
>   *en el tiempo pasado*
I succumb.
>   *sucumbo.*
moments pass
>   *los momentos pasan*
like hours---
>   *como las horas*

Remember me,
Oh, HOLY ONE!
    Recuérdame
    ¡Oh Sacrosanto!

"WE are ONE,
    Somos uno
Poet, you and I.
    tú y yo. poeta
Amused, and mused"
Divertidos y musativos

"WE dance, a dance
    danzamos una danza
Only you can hear!"
    que sólo tú puedes oír
Slowly, YOU invite me in
    Lentamente me invitas a entrar
release me, unstuck
    líbrame del atasco
my fingers now
    ahora mis dedos
are free to wonder
    son libres de preguntarse
in this cold abode,
    en esta fría morada
to join the mode
    para unirse al modo
of wedding guests
    de los invitados a la boda
around the floor,
    alrededor del suelo,
in circles turn,
    girando en círculos

while I discern,
    mientras yo discierno,
a piercing sound,
    el sonido penetrante,
from a chamber
    desde una cámara
in my heart,
    en mi corazón
Beating, louder
    Latiendo, más fuerte
through my chest...
    a través de mi pecho ...
a long last symphony,
    una sinfonia perdida,
I vaguely remanence.
    Yo vaga remanencia.
Exterior---pointed,
    Exterior puntiagudo,
with razor edges,
    con filos de navaja
Mary says.
    Dice Mary
Interior---languid
    lánguido interior
With dripping wedges
    Con cuñas que gotean
I say.
    Yo digo
YOU
    Tú
pull me deeper
    me llevas profundo
into your sanctum,
    a tu santuario

Into YOUR icy age
    a tu edad de hielo
Waves of Beauty BLUE.
    Ondas de belleza AZUL.

I surrender---close my eyes,
    Me rindo, cierro los ojos,
I am swimming---in a sea,
    Estoy nadando en un mar,
Mer Glacier!
    Mer Glacier!
I have arrived!
    He llegado
I am absorbed
    Estoy absorta
into HER womb
    en su vientre
I sense a trickle
    Siento un goteo
On my eyelid,
    En mi párpado
A melting teardrop
    Una lágrima que se derrite
Merging, fusing
    se fusiona, se funde,
With my own,
    Con mi lagrima misma,
Meltdown complete,
    completado el deshielo
I am re-born.
    Soy renacida
Frozen in my buoyant dream,
    Congelada en mi sueño boyante

I wake up suddenly,
> *Despierto de repente,*

To foot-steps drawing near.
> *A pasos que se acercan.*

Mine are stuck,
> *Los míos atascados*

Wedding guests
> *Invitados de boda*

mingle here and there,
> *se mezclan aquí y allá*

Mer Glacier,
> *Mer Glacier,*

Dis-appears.
> *Des-aparece.*

Where shall
> *a dónde*

we go
> *hemos de ir*

from here,
> *desde aquí,*

my wedding friends,
> *mis amigos de la boda,*

we are all married
> *casados todos*

to the Groom,
> *con el novio,*

with our carbon
> *con nuestra huella de carbono*

Footprints on the floor,
> *en el suelo*

Of Wedding Bride,
> *De la novia de la boda*

HER womb—wounded dearly so.
> *Su vientre malherido*

Hail Mary, full of GRACE
       Dios te salve María llena eres de Gracia,
Forgive us, not?
       nos perdonarás ¿no?
our sins are at the hour
       nuestros pecados están en la hora
of our death,
       de nuestra muerte,
beating away,
       cincelando
drop by drop
       gota a gota
My tears---my fears
       Mis lágrimas... mis miedos
Withering, even HOPE.
       Marchita, incluso la esperanza.

Hold me Mother
       Abrázame Madre
For we have sinned!
       Porque hemos pecado
I reach out.
       Extiendo la mano.

A Quiet silence echoes
       Un calmo silencio resuena
From the BLUE chamber glow.
       Desde el resplandor de la cámara AZUL.

As the Wedding Guests
       Mientras los invitados a la boda
Retreat from icy walls,
       se retiran de los gélidos muros

Blue-blocks of ice
    Bloques azules de hielo
Sheer Beauty
    Belleza pura
Stunned me cold,
    que fría me pasmó
Never had I
    Nunca había estado
been so ashamed,
    así de avergonzada
Never had we
    Nunca habíamos
Trespassed so erroneously!
    ¡Pasado tan erróneamente!

I pause—stand still
    Me pauso, quieta
A throb in the walls
    Un latido en las paredes
Pulse---calling me
    el Pulso, llamándome
FREEZE---
    Hiela

I am/ /was/ been
    soy/fuí/estuve
Time relent-less
    implacable tiempo
Marking on
    marcando
I cannot move--- on
    No puedo ir hacia--delante
This momentum
    Este impulso

Has no U-turn
>*No tiene vuelta en U*
We are/have/been
>*Somos/hemos/estado*
Mary and I
>*Mary y yo*
Witnesses---
>*testigos*
To your weeping walls.
>*De tus muros llorosos*

If they call me
>*Si me llaman*
To testify
>*Para testificar*
I will tell them
>*Les diré*
you were once---a *Sea!*
>*que una vez, Usted era... ¡un Mar!*

I am sorry,
>*Lo siento,*
We invaded YOUR
>*Hemos invadido*
Sacred *Sea,*
>*tu sagrado mar*
YOUR tears now
>*ahora tus lágrimas*
Unstoppable?
>*¿son imparables?*

Cutting through the hard rock,
>*Cortando la dura roca*

YOUR sapphire knife,
>	*Tu cuchillo de zafiro,*
gashes blocks of ice,
>	*tajos de bloques de hielo,*
Adding to a raging river,
>	*Agregando a un río embravecido*
through the valley, Chamonix
>	*por el valle de Chamonix*
One day, a village under siege.
>	*Un día, un pueblo bajo asedio*

Is it really the finale?
>	*¿Es realmente el final?*
End of the ice age, as they say.
>	*Fin de la edad de hielo, como dicen.*
Once a glacier,
>	*Una vez un glaciar,*
Stood here and firm---I will say.
>	*Se mantuvo aquí firme… diré.*

We will *sing* a ballad,
>	*Cantaremos una balada,*
in your name,
>	*en tu nombre*
an Ice Cave Beauty Blue,
>	*una cueva fría de bello azul*
once was here,
>	*una vez estuvo aquí,*
Of pinnacles
>	*De cumbres*
so sharp
>	*tan afilados*
they cut your gaze,
>	*que cortan tu mirada*

of languid walls,
 de lánguidas murallas
so smooth,
 tan suaves
they made you weep,
 que te hicieron llorar,
unsurpassed, was SHE.
 Ella era, insuperable,

Mer Glacier!
 Mer Glacier!

3²

El "Krack"*

El "Krack"*
Fue antes del amanecer
oído al rededor del mundo
Demoniaco temblor bailó girando
bajo una grieta del mar
nada menos que en la lejana Indonesia
la pálida oscuridad abrió la llave
Lo bello en la Bestia convocó a Mary,

Krack!

Su rostro surcado emergió
pavoroso
insondables abismos de fuego y hielo
ella escribió y forjó la cola de una criatura.
La noche entera, y hasta hoy no llega el día
aun el SOL quedó taciturno, afligido
tierra de ningún hombre, de ninguna mujer desierto de penumbras
acechando en el aire, resonando UNO

Krack!

Una ola perforó sus tímpanos
tintineo del ocaso
Mary dormitó un difícil sueño
Despierta sin lugar a dudas
La tierra cambiaba, la naturaleza empezaba a revelarse
¿A manos de un médico o de un técnico de laboratorio?

Krack!

Ella trama ojo pálido amarillo, con una simple onda eléctrica
para despertar sus miembros
Catástrofe, un desdichado monstruo nació,

Polaris se movió en el cielo haciendo espacio,

¿Qué había ella, Mary Wollstone, creado con esmero?
1819, su historia, revelada al mundo,
Las manos del Dr. Frankenstein
jugando en un laboratorio,
2019, nuestra historia comienza, donde ella
lo dejó,

Krack!

Covid-19 se escuchó en todo el mundo.

KRACK ("Key Reinstallation Attack") is a replay attack (a type of exploitable flaw) on the Wi-Fi Protected Access protocol that secures Wi-Fi connections. It was discovered in 2016 by the Belgian researchers Mathy Vanhoef and Frank Piessens of the University of Leuve.

33

Muda mutabilidad

Mary Shelley uses the term "mutability" only once in her travel diary in describing her encounter of a literary landmark of Rousseau.

"Here a small obelisk is erected to the glory of Rousseau, and here (such is the mutability of human life) the magistrates, the successors of those who exiled him from his native country, were shot by the populace during that revolution, which his writings mainly contributed to mature, and which, notwithstanding the temporary bloodshed and injustice with which it was polluted, has produced enduring benefits to mankind... (History of Six Weeks' Tour, p. 101)

However, she included the P. Shelley poem, "Mutability" in her novel *Frankenstein*. The following poem, "Muted Mutability" is based on fragments of poetry from Wordsworth, Coleridge and P. Shelley presented in *Frankenstein* and scientific abstracts about mutability. The lines of text were intermingled with my own poetic lines as a replay on the original texts---a poetic license. This idea of 'splicing' this poem was inspired by the scientific studies on "Spliceosome Dynamics" that used P. Shelley line--- *"Nought may endure but Mutability."*

Muted mutability
Muda mutabilidad
Shall never hang her cloak
nunca colgará su manto
On the shoulders,
sobre los hombros
Of the dwarfed
de los empequeñecidos
illuminati
iluminati
human shield.
escudos humanos.

Ghastly, and scarr'd, and riven.—Is this the scene
Abominable, con cicatrices y desgarrado. ¿Es esta la escena
Where the old Earthquake-daemon taught her young
Donde el viejo sismo diabólico instruyó a sus criaturas
Ruin? Were these their toys? or did a sea
la ruina? ¿Fueron esos sus juguetes? ¿O un mar
Of fire envelop once this silent snow?
De fuego una vez envolvió esta silenciosa nieve?

"As a mutation,
"Como mutación,
more likely
es más probable
to disrupt--- an interaction
alterar, una interacción
than to form---
que formar...
a new one,"
una nueva"

We rest;

Descansamos;

a dream has power--- to poison sleep.

un sueño tiene poder--- para envenenar el sueño

We rise;

Nos levantamos;

We feel, conceive, or reason;

sentimos, concebimos o razonamos;

laugh or weep,

reímos o lloramos,

Like one who, on a lonely road,

Como aquel que, en un camino solitario,

Doth walk in fear and dread,

avanza temeroso

Ghastly, obvious

Obviamente horrendo

doomed to ruin?

Condenado a la ruina

virus strikes the hour

el virus golpea la hora

reverberating

reverberando

from the bell towers

desde los campanarios

once, twice, thrice---

una, dos, tres veces...

ad infinitum?

ad infinitum?

from Notre Dame of Paris

desde Notre Dame de París

to St. Peter's of New York

hasta San Pedro de Nueva York

ringing in my ear---

sonando en mi oído...

an echo heard 'round the world,
un eco se escuchó por todo el mundo
on one forgotten day,
en un día olvidado,
December 2020.
Diciembre 2020

From yon remotest waste, have overthrown
Desde los residuos más remotos, han derribado
The limits of the dead and living world,
Los límites entre el mundo de vivos y muertos
Never to be reclaimed. The dwelling-place
Nunca será reclamado. La morada
Of insects, beasts, and birds, becomes its spoil;
De insectos, bestias y aves,
se vuelve su despojo

"It is likely
"Es probable
that relative stabilization
que una relativa estabilización
takes the form of destabilization,
tome la forma de desestabilización,

Embrace fond woe, or cast our cares away;
Abraza al infortunio, o desecha nuestras penas;
one wand'ring thought pollutes the day.
un vago pensamiento contamina el día.

Their food and their retreat for ever gone,
Su comida y su refugio por siempre idos

So much of life and joy is lost. The race
Se ha perdido gran parte de la vida y la alegría.

Of man, flies far in dread his work and dwelling
La raza de los hombres, vuela lejos en el pavor de su trabajo y morada

Vanish, like smoke before the tempest's stream.
Desaparece, como humo ante el torrente de la tempestad.

of the competing
de la competencia
conformation,
conformidad

And, having once turned round, walks on
Y, una vez que, dada la vuelta, camina
And turns no more his head;
y no gires más la cabeza

It is the same: for, be it joy or sorrow,
Si lo mismo es: que sea alegría o pesar
The path of its departure still is free.
La senda por la que se fue aún es libre

And their place is not known. Below, vast caves
Y su lugar se desconoce. Abajo, vastas cuevas
Shine in the rushing torrent's restless gleam,
Brillan en el inquieto resplandor del torrente,
Which from those secret chasms in tumult welling
Que desde esos secretos abismos brotan en tumulto
Meet in the vale, and one majestic River,
se congregan en el valle, del Río majestuoso

Because he knows a frightful fiend
Porque él conoce un espantoso demonio
Doth close behind him tread.
que le acecha desde atrás.

Early February 2021,
Principios de febrero de 2021,
church bells 'nought endure',
las campanas de la iglesia "no resisten",
ceased to ring upon the hour,
dejaron de sonar la hora,
cease to ring at all.
paran de sonar en absoluto.

The breath and blood of distant lands, for ever
El aliento y la sangre de lejanas tierras, para siempre
Rolls its loud waters to the ocean waves,
rueda sus recias aguas hacia las olas del océano
Breathes its swift vapours to the circling air.
Exhala sus rápidos vapores al aire circundante

None can reply—all seems eternal now.
Nadie puede responder: todo parece eterno ahora.
The wilderness has a mysterious tongue
La tierra salvaje tiene una lengua misteriosa
Which teaches awful doubt, or faith so mild,
Que enseña la duda horrible, o la fe tan suave,

No more willing,
Sin más voluntad,
To attend---not even daring dwarfs
Para vigilar… siquiera a los enanos atrevidos
Human shields lay at the door,
Los escudos humanos yacen en la puerta,
No longer restless,
Ya no están inquietos,
Only still.
Sino en calma

Beneath the sacred arches,
Bajo los arcos sagrados,
Silently, the ghosts exhale,
silenciosamente, los fantasmas exhala
swift vapours to the circling air
rápidos vapores al aire circundanter

"At present, however,
"Sin embargo, en el presente
molecular basis of the action,
la base molecular de la acción,

So solemn, so serene, that man may be,
Tan solemne, tan sereno, que podría ser hombre
But for such faith, with Nature reconciled
Aunque para semejante fe, con la Naturaleza reconciliada;

of these general suppressor
de estos supresores generales
mutations--- is unknown."
mutaciones... es desconocido

Man's yesterday may ne'er be like his morrow;
Quizás el ayer del hombre nunca sea como su mañana
Nought may endure but mutability!
Lo único que perdura es lo mutable

Infiniti---Illuminati
Infinati---Iluminati
Do we dare ask?
¿Nos atrevemos a preguntar?
When shall Thee, Creator mine,
Cuando habrás de hacerlo vos, mi Creador?

'Shine in the rushing torrent'
Brillan en el inquieto torrente,
To mute the mutability?
Para inmutar la mutabilidad?

Rosalinda Ruiz Scarfuto, 2019

References

1. Bennett (2010). Screening Approaches to Identify Genes Required for DNA Double-Strand Break Damage Signaling in the Yeast Saccharomyces cerevisiae" in Handbook of Cell Signaling, Chapter 260: Academic Press, p. 2145-2158). "Screening Approaches to Identify Genes Required for DNA Double-Strand Break Damage Signaling in the Yeast Saccharomyces cerevisiae"

2. Coleridge, Samuel Taylor. "The Rime of the Ancient Mariner".

3. Country Walkers (2020) Blog, Mont Blanc, History: "Modern mountaineering traces its roots back to 1760, when Swiss naturalist Horace Benedict de Saussure arrived in the Chamonix Valley and couldn't believe the beauty and magnitude of Mont Blanc rising above him."

4. Duncan J. Smith, Charles C. Query, Maria M. Konarska (2008) "'Nought May Endure but Mutability': Spliceosome Dynamics and the Regulation of Splicing", in Molecular Cell, Volume 30, Issue 6.

5. Duncan, et al. (2008) "Nought May Endure but Mutability": Spliceosome Dynamics and the Regulation of Splicing", in Molecular Cell 30, June 20, (660-666): Abstract: "Assembly can be stimulated or repressed by the binding of general or specific splicing factors to snRNPs and pre-mRNA. snRNPs can also interact both with pre-mRNA and with each other. Spliceosome assembly is, thus, highly cooperative, and the fact that many interactions can occur independently of one another results in

an assembly cascade that does not follow a single obligatory trajectory but instead can occur via multiple pathways."

6. Ford, T. (2009). Mary Wollstonecraft and the Motherhood of Feminism. *Women's Studies Quarterly*, 37(3/4), 189-205. Retrieved January 27, 2021.

7. Ford, T. (2009). Mary Wollstonecraft and the Motherhood of Feminism. Women's Studies Quarterly, 37(3/4), 189-205. Retrieved January 27, 2021.

8. Gilbert, A., C. Vincent, O. Gagliardini, J. Krug and E. Berthier (2015). Assessment of thermal change in cold avalanching glaciers in relation to climate warming, Geophys. Lett., 42.

9. Hogsette, D. (2011). Metaphysical Intersections in "Frankenstein": Mary Shelley's Theistic Investigation of Scientific Materialism and Transgressive Autonomy. *Christianity and Literature, 60*(4), 531-559. Retrieved January 29, 2021.

10. Juneau, K., Palm, C., Miranda, M., and Davis, R.W. (2007). "High-density yeasttiling array reveals previously undiscovered introns and extensive regulation of meiotic splicing," in Proc. Natl. Acad. Sci. USA 104, 1522–1527.

11. Kaur, S. P., & Gupta, V. (2020). "COVID-19 Vaccine: A comprehensive status report," in Virus research, Volume 288, 15 October 2020, 198114.

12. Nicholson, M. (2020). A Singular Experiment: Frankenstein's Creature and the Nature of Scientific Community. Science Fiction Studies, 47(1), 1-29.

13. Shelley, M. (1817). History of a six weeks' tour, Introduction. Mary uses the term 'husband' only twice in the travel diary introduction. In the remaining pages (183 total), she uses the word 'companion'.

14. Shelley, M. (1817). *History of a six weeks' tour: Through a part of France, Switzerland, Germany and Holland with letters descriptive of a sail round the Lake of Geneva, and of the glaciers of Chamouni,* London: Hookham.

15. Shelley, M. (1819). *Frankenstein,* See online version: The Project

Gutenberg eBook of Frankenstein, by Mary Wollstonecraft (Godwin) Shelley.

16. Shelley, Percy Bysshe (1814) "Mont Blanc".

17. Shelley, Percy Bysshe. "Mutability".

18. Steiner, R. (1997 ed.) *The Ahrimanic Deception,* Schmidt Number: S-3889 On-line since: 23rd October, 1997.

19. Tomaselli, Sylvana, (2020). "Mary Wollstonecraft" in The Stanford Encyclopedia of Philosophy (Winter 2020 Edition), Edward N. Zalta (ed.). "When Wollstonecraft came to write The Vindication of the Rights of Woman, which she did within a matter of months following the publication of her first overtly political work, the moral rejuvenation of society and the happiness of individual women were woven together. It argues that women should be taught skills so as to be able to support themselves and their children in widowhood, and never have to marry or remarry out of financial necessity. It seeks to reclaim midwifery for women, against the encroachment of men into this profession, and contends that women could be physicians just as well as nurses. It urges women to extend their interests to encompass politics and the concerns of the whole of humanity. In Wollstonecraft's view, marriages ought to have friendship rather than physical attraction as their basis Kendrick (2019)."

20. US Geological Society, (2010) Volcanoes, Tambora 1815. "Before its eruption in 1815, Tambora might have been in repose for as much as 5,000 years (Barberi and others, 1983). At least 6 months and probably about 3 years of increased steaming and small phreatic eruptions preceded the 1815 Tambora eruption, the largest in historical time...A moderately large explosive eruption occurred on 5 April 1815, from which ash fell in east Java and thunder like sounds were heard up to 1,400 kilometers away."

21. Vargo, L. J., Anderson, B. M., Dadić, R. et al. (2020) Anthropogenic warming forces extreme annual glacier mass loss," in Nature Climate Change,10, 856–861. Abstract: "Here we apply event attribution methods to document this at the regional scale,

targeting the highest mass-loss years (2011 and 2018) across New Zealand's Southern Alps. We estimate extreme mass loss was at least six times (2011) and ten times (2018) (>90% confidence) more likely to occur with anthropogenic forcing than without. This increased likelihood is driven by present-day temperatures ~1.0 °C above the pre-industrial average, confirming a connection between anthropogenic emissions and high annual ice loss. These results suggest that as warming and extreme heat events continue and intensify, there will be an increasingly visible human fingerprint on extreme glacier mass-loss years in the coming decades."

Selfie Mont Blanc
R. Ruiz Scarfuto 2019

Dr. Rosalinda Ruiz Scarfuto, poet-painter, completed her doctoral thesis on the Forest Flaneur methodology in 2018 in the UK. Previously, her Masters was based on literary routes inspired by nature obtained from University of Alcala, Spain. Her degree in Social Ecology from the University of California adds value to her perspective on the environmental aspects of her work. Art courses and workshops from Japan to Spain have accompanied her process over several decades including ceramics, wood block printing, abstract painting and jazz music. The colour palette of a poetic canvas is the culmination of a visual-tactile perception based on slow walks in rural areas. Past studies of poetic landscapes included classic and contemporary writers. One of her 3D poetic canvases is part of Gary Snyder's private collection. Calabi Gallery in Santa Rosa, California represents Rosalinda. *Musings at Mont Blanc; with Mary Shelley Wollstonecraft* is part of a new series of poetic canvases dedicated to women artists. For more information visit: forestflanuer.com or re-bound.org to contact Rosalinda.